THE GENIUS
MACHINE

THE GENIUS MACHINE

{ **THE 11 STEPS THAT TURN RAW IDEAS INTO BRILLIANCE** }

GERALD SINDELL

New World Library
Novato, California

New World Library
14 Pamaron Way
Novato, California 94949

Copyright © 2009 by Gerald Sindell

Text design by Tona Pearce Myers

Library of Congress Cataloging-in-Publication Data
Sindell, Gerald Seth.
The genius machine : the eleven steps that turn raw ideas into brilliance / Gerald Sindell.
    p.   cm.
Includes index.
ISBN 978-1-57731-650-3 (hardcover : alk. paper)
1. New products. 2. Product management. 3. Marketing. 4. Critical thinking—Popular works. I. Title.
HF5415.153S57 2009
658.5'75—dc22   2009002429

First printing, April 2009
ISBN 978-1-57731-650-3
Printed in Canada on 100% postconsumer-waste recycled paper

g New World Library is a proud member of the Green Press Initiative.

10   9   8   7   6   5   4   3   2   1

For Leanne, beloved muse, mate, partner, agent

{ CONTENTS }

{ INTRODUCTION }

What Is Thinking?

My work is to help people think. My clients write books, create innovative solutions, develop brilliant breakthroughs, and endeavor to make the world a better place.

One of the great challenges in getting new and valuable ideas accepted is that many intended users, even those who would benefit enormously from what is being offered, spend a lot of energy and time trying to figure out who the person is behind the innovation. Until we feel comfortable that we know the answer, it's hard for us to accept advice, no matter how valuable it might be. I often suggest to my clients that they help their intended users get past this barrier by being as explicit about themselves as they can be, as soon as they can. This goes for companies too. We're Acme, we stand for discovering the colors that will bring joy to your life. Okay, got it: Acme equals colors of joy. Now I can forget about you and look at your palette.

So let's get me out of the way: I'm a guy in my early sixties who was in the film business for the first decade and a half of his professional life, who then migrated to book publishing. In film, as a director, writer, and editor, I learned about pacing and storytelling. And as an entrepreneur, I learned about being creative on time and within a budget.

When my brother and I made our first full-length feature motion picture, *Double-Stop*, I was constantly haunted by the fear that the moment we finished the film's principal photography, and the cast and crew dispersed, I would suddenly come up with some brilliant idea that should have been part of the movie but now never could be. That concern stayed with me, and it guides all the intellectual property development I engage in, including the development of this book. We must have our brilliant ideas *now*, in the development stage. Fully developing our best ideas after our work has gone into production or to market is way too late.

I also learned how to market movies from some of

the best people in the business. As a publisher and book developer, I employed those same skills to help authors become better storytellers, and to find better ways to get new and valuable information into the marketplace of ideas.

During the last twenty years of working with business leaders to build their personal reputations, and to enhance the profile of their organizations, I created a system for developing intellectual property — ideas. Not long ago a number of my clients turned the tables on me and suggested I take a little of my own medicine and organize my methodology. I eventually distilled my process down to eleven essential steps. I wrote a draft outline and circulated it among many of my clients, asking if it captured what they had found valuable. With their comments and further refinement, that system is what you now hold in your hands. I call it the Endleofon (END-leo-fahn), an old English word for "eleven," and some of my clients call it the Genius Machine.

Using this process, I have helped dozens of authors create books that have sold many millions of copies. I have helped leaders in many fields learn to articulate their core knowledge so they could better share it with others. Recently I worked with one of the top two Internet companies to help them complete the development of a core knowledge area, and to turn that into a book that may soon help millions of people all over the globe. What's so good about the Endleofon system? It's fast, it's complete, it helps people quickly get to the bottom of what they need to think through, and it anticipates the outreach part of innovation at the very beginning. It is not unusual for an individual or group working with the process to suddenly realize that they can speed through a development cycle in days, not months or years. And with the Endleofon, innovations are always developed with the understanding that it's tough to get new ideas accepted.

What else do you need to know about me so we can get started? Simply, I am driven to deliver valuable knowledge and ideas to the people who would benefit from that knowledge. Whether this means a subsistence farmer trying to increase his yield, a Swiss banker needing a fresh view of the global economy, or a young person anywhere trying to figure out how to plan a satisfying life, I am eager to diffuse ideas and to improve the process of diffusion. The terrible gap that lies between existing knowledge and the persistence of ignorance — and its concomitant poverty, illness, and suffering — drives me crazy.

Enough about me. Let's start thinking!

What is thinking? Some thinking is actually contemplation — thinking about something you'd like to eat or a place you might like to visit someday. Some thinking is problem solving — two trains, each carrying twelve penguins, leave Philadelphia at the same time traveling in opposite directions. How will the penguins get back in touch?

This book is about a third kind of thinking, one that is directed toward improving an existing idea, thinking through a complete issue, or creating something new. We use this kind of thinking when we're designing a house, creating a better way for people in our company to work together, or coming up with a better method for kids to learn something. This kind of thinking is about creating something with a particular goal in mind. If we're successful, we'll have a better toaster, a better company, a better school system, a better way to choose political leaders.

Imagine how the world would be if everyone could be really smart when they needed to be. The best ideas would always be the ones we'd choose to use, we'd find great solutions for all our problems, organizations would reflect the best values of its employees more often than not, and the world would be one wonderful place to live.

The kind of creative thinking encouraged by the Endleofon is not about simply choosing from various alternatives. If a particular existing choice answers the need perfectly, then fine, we should choose it. But creative thinking is also capable of helping us quickly see when the existing choices aren't good enough and that we need to develop something better.

Creative thinking has had some pretty good results so far. It has yielded the wheel, democracy, the Internet, and Morbier cheese, with the morning milk on the bottom and the afternoon milk on top, separated by a layer of wood ash. Brilliant! One might assume that, since this kind of thinking is so valuable, there's probably a pretty well-established way to go about it already out there. And yet surprisingly, there is no generally accepted system for creative thinking. Put a bunch of people in a room and ask them to solve a complex problem, and the first thing they're going to do is create a process for solving the problem, because there isn't one on the shelf, ready to use.

What did you learn in school about creative thinking? Most really creative kids get directed into an art class if they want to express themselves. How about math? Did you learn creative ways to solve problems there? Most of us learned a prescribed way to solve math problems and to come up with the right answer. How many "creative" projects did you have in all of high school? How about in college and beyond? Even if you pursued a PhD, you may have found that creativity is generally channeled into the narrowest of purposes — to move the knowledge in your chosen field a few inches farther. That's how academic knowledge works. It's not surprising, then, that learning how to think creatively in an organized process is simply not an important part of our formal education.

Then comes the real world. In order to develop ourselves, for our companies to flourish, and for our world to improve, we need to be able to think creatively, not just solve problems. We require the ability to create brilliant new solutions, to invent what has never existed before. In the real world, the most valued skills are the ones for which we have little training and no rulebook. Even when we have a pretty good new idea, we don't have a ready system to guide us in developing, testing, and refining it and then stepping back and seeing whether, underneath it all, we've come up with something that's just a little new, or something really, really important.

I hope the Endleofon will change that. It's a system that can help you get from the beginning of a problem — whether it be a complex one that needs solving or a brilliant vision that needs filling out — to the point where your work is fully developed and ready to take its rightful place in the world.

I have structured this book to be as useful and as linear as possible, despite the fact that thinking tends to be circular. The book is designed for straightforward navigation, so that, having read it through once, you will be able to jump easily to a useful spot whenever you desire a refresher. The Endleofon begins with *distinctions* and ends with *advocacy*. I hope you'll find that advocacy leads you right back to making new and valuable distinctions!

CHAPTER ONE

{ DISTINCTIONS }

Yes, There Is No Vanilla

A genius thinker looks at what everyone else has
looked at and sees something new.

Innovation begins with a need — whether it's the next-generation high-speed switch, a change in corporate culture, the design for a flagship product, or finishing a book on deadline. Throughout our lives we are met with challenges to create something that isn't already there. We can either do decent work and make something that, at the very least, does the job, or we can come up with something that is simply brilliant.

In many ways, the choice is yours. A great many people get by with doing a pedestrian job of it. But many of us would like to create something that truly reflects our potential. Certainly, if we're consultants trying to make a living by being the smartest person on the block, brilliant work helps our bottom line. And for the rest of us — those of us working in organizations, researching in science, struggling for a PhD, or just pursuing our dreams — knowing how to think brilliantly could make all the difference in how we experience our lives.

The process we're about to explore has lifted a great number of people to function at their genius level. This process has generated books that not only have fulfilled the lives of a lot of authors but also have transformed the world's largest organizations. In helping draw brilliance from a few, this process has improved the lives of hundreds of thousands, if not millions, of people.

Here's the structure of the Endleofon: We start by recognizing that you have work to do, an idea to be developed, a problem to be solved, a notion that needs to be ferreted out and developed. We'll start at the beginning, with what real thinking is, and then I'm going to lead you through all kinds of interesting and even challenging processes, until not only are your ideas fully developed but also your work will be aligned with your life's goals. Successful development of your ideas will mean that what you create also helps fulfill your life. This is true too for people working in teams. Your team will get to the truth of your values as a group and as members of a larger organization, and your work will be aligned with what you want to do as individuals, as a team, and as part of that organization.

Since genius thinking requires integrities of vision, mission, and self-knowledge, we must accept that not all individuals, teams, or organizations are going to easily achieve the alignment required to do great work. If fundamental disagreements about values exist either within a team or between the team and the larger organization, success may require that some people leave this particular effort. If as you work through the Endleofon process, disagreements surface that cannot be resolved, don't attempt to paper them over.

Defining Your Point of Departure

The first step in the process of discovery is stating what it is we're trying to do. Throughout this book you'll find lots of examples and stories that we'll examine once and not revisit. But I thought it might be worthwhile to create three examples that repeat throughout the book to show how the eleven steps can bring robust innovation. The three examples that we will return to repeatedly are designing an eco-friendly toaster, finding the best way to educate children, and developing a way to stem the flow of talented people leaving our organization.

With each of these projects, we need to make sure that we're stating the root of what we're trying to do, and not just addressing a symptom. Let's take the eco-friendly toaster. We need to ask what problem an eco-friendly toaster will solve. Do we want to reduce the total carbon impact of our toasters, from manufacture, to fuel consumption, to recycling? Or are we simply trying to create this toaster to appeal to a customer who would like to believe that buying an eco-friendly toaster would be a good thing to do for the earth? Depending on the answer, we might come up with significantly different solutions.

How about the desire to discover the "best way" to educate children? We will need to decide what age group we're going to focus on. And we're going to need to figure out what we mean by "best way," by defining a specific series of measures that will let us see differences between one way and another.

In our effort to find a way to stem the flow of talented people from our organization, our first challenge might be to find the reason why talented people are leaving the organization. Then we can begin to develop possible solutions.

When we state our challenge, we must define our time constraints. Do we have one week or five years to develop our solution? A realistic budget for time will help us decide when to end the divergence part of our work — the phase when we look at all kinds of possibilities and directions — and when we will need to begin narrowing our options.

We must also, as individuals or as a group, describe what success will look like in a number of time frames: in one year, three years, five years.

THINKING IS MAKING DISTINCTIONS

To a surprising extent, thinking is a matter of making distinctions. If we do not see the differences among various kinds of lettuce, for instance, our understanding of a salad will be limited to the perception that it's just a bunch of green stuff in a bowl. But if you were a truck farmer in Ohio specializing in growing boutique greens for the New York and Chicago restaurant markets, you would be familiar with dozens of lettuces. You would know their growing preferences, their pests, their various flavors at different stages of growth. You would know when to pick them, how to pack them, how to ship them, and how to price them.

Take a moment to think about "white." Without making distinctions, one might say that white is simply white. But take a piece of white paper, or gaze at a white wall for a moment. What do you really see when you look at white? On my desk, my white sheet of paper is resting on a yellow legal pad. When I raise or lower the white sheet, I can see the yellow cast from below and even some faint green lines. If I let my eyes rest on the whitest part of the white sheet, I see lots of dancing blue areas and considerable gray blotchiness moving around.

Then it dawns on me that *movement* is the most prominent aspect of seeing white. For a moment I recollect being a child, looking at a perfect blue sky (a rarity in Cleveland, so when it happened, you took the time to stare), and wondering if everyone else saw a million dancing little objects in what was supposed to be just flat blue. After contemplating the effect for several years, I began to realize that the pointillism I was seeing was more likely a characteristic of my eyes than something in the sky. Another distinction.

To help you develop your appetite for making distinctions, you might consider spending a day in a museum just looking at various artists' use of white. Renoir frequently used white to show the dazzle effect of bright sun. You can imagine him using white as the last pass he made at a canvas. His whites are always on top, used in tiny areas, to convey the glint of a bright sun on grasses and other greenery. Van Gogh's whites, on the other hand, are like the rest of his colors: swirls of high energy with the underpainting always peeking through.

Have vanilla ice cream in your fridge? When you have a moment, take it out. Taste it. Think about what it actually tastes like. Does it taste like burnt sugar? Does the taste change as it fades away on your tongue? Does the taste alter as it gets warmer in your mouth? Now take a second spoonful. Is the impression of the second taste more intense or less intense than the first? Next time you go to the market, buy three or four kinds of vanilla ice cream. Taste them side by side. Perceive the differences. Try to describe the differences so that someone else might be able to understand what it is you're tasting.

The same is true for ideas. If you are thinking about a problem you want to solve, or something you want to convey to others, you'll find it valuable to express what you actually see and think. There are no vanilla ideas. There is no plain old white or black. Everything is dazzle and movement. Uniqueness is there, waiting to be witnessed and captured.

Creative thought is about looking at what everyone is looking at, or has looked at for years, and seeing something new. Sometimes that new thing is just the possibility of something new, and sometimes what we see is right there, already in existence, but had never been noticed before. Charles Goodyear noticed that natural gum rubber charred like leather when it was heated but didn't burn up. He thought he had discovered something important, that rubber might be able to be "cured," but when he brought his observations to others in his brother's nearly bankrupt rubber factory, where they were working only with pure fresh rubber, no one was interested. Eventually his discovery contributed one of the essential elements of the modern industrial era.

Seeing, as opposed to looking, is the beginning of

thinking. The challenge is to see through our own eyes and not through the preconceptions we may have developed from what others have told us, or from what we have gathered unconsciously. Ever ask someone about a movie recently seen and heard the answer "I didn't expect to like it, but it was pretty good"? If we have expectations, it makes it more difficult for us to actually see.

In the biblical narrative of creation, the opening verses of Genesis give us a powerful view of the significance of making distinctions, of seeing. Genesis says that at first everything was the same. "When God began to create heaven and the earth — the earth being unformed and void" — the first thing God did was call for light, and then God separated the light from the darkness. Next God divided the sky from the earth, and then separated the land from the water. Distinction after distinction is made in the void, until the earth is fully populated with a vast variety of plants and creatures. The story of Creation is the story of making separations, of making distinctions.

This is the essence of the new, a continuing refinement of what is, into ever greater variety and possibility. Consider the last five or so centuries of music. Think of Gregorian chants, sung one note at a time, simple harmony or no harmony, straightforward rhythms. Then consider the development of music over the centuries, complex tonal modalities and harmonies, ever more complicated rhythmic discoveries, cultural influences swirling together into an ever more varied and remarkable soup.

COMPLEXITY CREATES SIMPLICITY

Running in the direction opposite of ever more complexity is our preference for more surface simplicity. We want our computer operating systems to become so simple that they're virtually invisible to us. In the old days of DOS, a user needed to know dozens of commands to make the computer load a program and work. Now, with a vast operating system made up of millions of lines of code, a user hardly knows it's there. So the antidote for inevitably ever greater complexity, as we continue to see and create never-ending new distinctions, is our ever increasing preference for the elegance found in apparent simplicity. Without elegance, we would drown in the very real complexity that underlies all our technologies.

In engineering, elegance means that a solution has been achieved with less — less force, less energy, less material, fewer parts. Ben Franklin was a particularly elegant inventor. His solution to a person's need for close-vision glasses and distant-vision glasses was the invention of the bifocal lens. People no longer had to constantly shift between two pairs of glasses. Franklin's solution to the endless threat of building fires caused by lightning strikes was also elegant. The inelegant solution was to build buildings far apart, so if one caught fire, the neighboring structures would be spared. Huge water supplies would have to be kept nearby to fight fires. Slate roofs were helpful, and brick or stone could replace wood. All these solutions were expensive in terms of time and materials. Franklin's solution cost a few pennies and took only the slightest effort. First, one had to provide a slightly higher and more attractive target for lightning (by fastening a metal post — the lightning rod — to the roof). Second, one had to establish a path by which the energy would bypass the building and go directly into the ground (the grounding wire).

Elegance is inherently attractive: simplicity is artful. In thinking and writing, too, elegance is appealing. When we have refined our thinking to the point that our hard work has become invisible, then we will have achieved elegance. Elegant thinking has many advantages over its cruder competition: elegance communicates more efficiently, is likely to be adopted faster, and will often have the strength to fend off the competition. Elegance is not only good ideas well thought through but also good ideas cleaned up and well dressed. Elegant thinking is much more likely to be invited in.

In our creative thinking, at first we create new complexity as we make more distinctions. And as we explore the inevitable new complexity that is part of the creative process, many of us will become anxious that what we're creating is too complex, too cumbersome, too awkward, too expensive to ever be accepted or useful. But trust that once we've fully explored our new creation, the next stage of the process will be refinement toward elegance. The achievement of elegance is one of the ways we'll know we're done.

Think about the cars we drive now and compare them to the vehicles of the early days of the horseless carriage. These early vehicles had extremely simple systems for suspension, for steering (a bar straight out of a horse-drawn wagon), and for braking. The total number of distinct parts in a 1903 Duryea was fewer than twenty-two hundred, and driving it required a week of training. A modern vehicle is comprised of more than ten thousand parts (not to mention tens of thousands of lines of code), and yet we can move from one type of car to another without even thinking about taking more than a moment to find the controls for the headlights and windshield wipers.

THE NECESSARY LEVEL OF GRANULARITY

At some point we will need to stop making distinctions, the process of seeing the new, and begin development, the process of organizing and refining our innovations. How do we know when we've gone far enough?

From predigital photography comes the metaphor

of granularity. Before digital, pictures were recorded by exposing silver halide crystals to light. The more crystals available on the original camera negative, the more information we could record. The same notion, applied to different technology, is true in digital photography. *Granularity* simply refers to how many receptors are available to record information, so that when we enlarge a picture to see details more clearly, we are able to reveal more and more of the information we originally captured. If you take a picture with your cell phone and try to make a billboard out of it, you're probably going to be disappointed with the results — there's enough information for you to see and understand the image when it's two inches wide, but when you blow it up to forty feet, something will be missing. Your image will probably not be sufficiently fine-grained to make sense on your larger canvas.

Granularity can be important when you are trying to develop something, as well as when you are deciding how much of what you have developed will be necessary for your ultimate user to know. If you are just grazing the web for news, you are probably going to be satisfied with a low-resolution take on what's happening at the moment. But if you are learning something that you will soon be teaching others, or gathering knowledge that you plan to build on, you will need a much higher level of detail — much more information than the person you will be teaching. Your job will be to select what's important from all the things you know.

The Delight of the Amateur

Granularity becomes a consideration when we're making judgments about useful distinctions. In virtually everything we do, we can always see more, learn more, capture more, dig more into any object or idea. We could spend the rest of our lives just getting to an incomplete but thorough understanding of white. Knowing everything about everything is probably impossible, given the time constraints of a human life, so understanding how fine-grained our knowledge of a subject must be puts some useful limits on us as we make distinctions. How do we determine the granularity needed in a given project? First, let the depth of your curiosity be your guide. If you are passionate about something, you will want to dig and dig until you have mastered a certain level of knowledge about your subject. English gentlefolk of the Victorian era often developed a passion for a specific area of knowledge and pursued it with lifelong devotion. They frequently did so without a college degree, and many poured their fortunes into their pursuits, as opposed to doing it for money. The word that described them best was *amateur*, which implies doing something "for the love of it."

A life shaped by the pursuit of knowledge, and

motivated by love for a specific subject, is often a happy one. But when you are creating something for another user, either by yourself or as part of a creative team, at some point you must develop it into something others can use. Whether you are creating a teaching methodology, a new energy source, or a user interface, your intended user is likely to be less passionate than you about what underlies your creation, and probably does not need to know everything that went into it. Overwhelming your intended user will hinder the adoption of your creation, no matter how brilliant or useful it might be.

Thinking is both about making distinctions and about being able to communicate those distinctions using the appropriate amount of granularity, determined by the simple guide of giving people just enough information so that they can use what you have created.

Developing Alternative Solutions

Here is the moment of major guessing. We need to take a look at our refined statement of what it is we're trying to solve or create, and develop a number of most-likely solutions. Some of these will fall by the wayside before too long, some may surprise us, and the ultimate solution or creation may not even be in our view yet. But we will need to start somewhere. It's important to explore alternate possibilities right from the beginning.

For our toaster challenge, we might imagine the

solution could be a solar-powered toaster. Others might suggest a chemical toaster, one that entails a reaction between the toast and the toaster that creates heat, possibly using the fuel contained within the bread itself. Some might imagine a wind-powered toaster, a methane-fueled toaster, a toaster that runs off of captured heat from some other source, such as a furnace, a fireplace, auto exhaust, or a treadmill.

In our education challenge, we might play with the possibilities of several existing education modalities, such as classrooms in which students are organized according to age or talent, and compare a strict curriculum to one that is child-centered. We might look at the potential of homeschooling, and even at some kind of experiential system, computer delivered or even subliminal.

For our employee-retention challenge, we'll want to discover whether the root cause of our high turnover is our culture, location, compensation, industry, competition, current recruiting issues, leadership, or something else. Until we've discovered the cause, it will be premature to imagine possible solutions.

DEFINITION OF SUCCESS

Finally, the last part of understanding our challenge is to ask ourselves, "If we are successful in what we are trying to achieve, what will success look like?" How can we tell that we have succeeded in our toaster development? How will we know that we have devised the best possible way to educate children? How will we know that we have solved the problem of retaining our most talented individuals?

The Endleofon innovation process cannot work without purpose. Without a direction to head toward, without an end result in sight, without a problem that needs solving, the innovation will be rudderless and will wander all over the ocean. As we progress in our thinking, then, we will need to revisit our definition of success and make sure we are still headed toward it. Our definition of success will be a valuable guide for the hundreds of decisions that make up the creative process. When I was a member of the board of an arts academy, one board member kept us all on track by occasionally asking the same simple question, "Is this good for the kids?" Our goal was to nourish young artists. The question kept us aligned with our goal.

If we define success inaccurately, we face the danger of achieving the wrong success. Imagine we are building a race car. If we define our goal as going faster, then everything we do will be aligned with whatever it takes to inch up our speed. But if we define our goal as winning races, then we will embrace everything involved, from suspension, to driver vision, to endurance.

Our definition of success needs to be revisited from

time to time. While we are working, creating, and innovating, the world also moves on. The goals we set at the beginning of a project begin to age from the moment we set them. Every few weeks or months, we need to determine whether what we have been working toward is tied to a time and context that no longer exist. Fuel costs can change everything. Tastes change. Other innovations create a constantly evolving environment. The intended audience we began with may not be the same audience that we will be trying to reach when we're ready to go to market.

Finally, not only will our intended user change, but also our project itself will change as we develop it. As we move along on our project, we will also need to determine whether our definition of success needs to expand or contract. Perhaps our original goals were overly ambitious and we can now see that we cannot possibly reach all of our initial goals with this particular project. It is also possible that our breakthroughs have been so audacious that we can expand our horizons, do more for our user than we had originally hoped, or reach a larger audience.

CHAPTER TWO

{ IDENTITY }

The Skinny Sumo

Genius thinkers know who they are
and what they are driven to contribute.

W hat do I stand for? As a creative team, what
do we stand for? Do we understand what
values we share, and do we understand the
identity of the organization we are part of? Is what we
are creating coherent with that identity? Will making
our identity as a group explicit help introduce our idea?

Who am I? Who are we? Why are these ideas important to me, and why am I driven to share them with the
world?

Now that we have said what it is we want to do, and even speculated a little about what possible alternatives we might turn up, now's the time to get clear on exactly who we are. Brilliant thinking does not take place unattached to a thinker. Thoughts have a pedigree. Brilliant thinking requires understanding who is doing the thinking, and understanding how what is being created relates to the values of the thinker. Since we are the thinkers here, we need to know ourselves.

There are two forces at work in creative thinking: first is the problem or challenge to be developed, which after a while can take on the force of a living being. A test jet engine, for example, may become a "she," and "her" quirks may grow in stature as we refine her performance. The second force is the person or group wrestling with the development.

What about the personification of ourselves, the people creating that engine, or you, trying to bring fresh thinking to reducing traffic in your city? What is your identity, and why is it important to know?

I had the privilege of working with author Larry Ackerman as he began to develop his first book on the natural laws of human identity, *Identity Is Destiny*. In it, Ackerman shared his discovery of what he calls the "Laws of Identity." From that time forward I have used Ackerman's insights into identity with every person and group I've worked with. I learned that, when we get to the truth of our own individual identity, and if we can figure out some things that are true about our identity as a group, we will have a powerful platform on which to build our ideas. Eventually we will have a fine yardstick with which to measure the fidelity of our creation to our goals.

The word *identity* has many meanings. But in the Endleofon process, *identity* means the part of us that is our absolute rock bottom. Our identity is the fingerprint of our soul, the part of us that is unchanging, or — to use an even lovelier word — immutable. Identity is the source of that feeling deep inside us that says we have something we were meant to do in the world, and that if we could just find it, we'd be on the right path. Fortunately, we *can* find it.

To make an important distinction here, the concept of individual identity is often confused with the concept of affiliation: I'm a Yalie, I'm a seventh-generation Mason, I'm French. Affiliations we acquire by birth or by choice can tell a little about ourselves, but if we think our affiliations are who we are, we will be missing the much more fundamental truths about our own uniqueness. Affiliations ultimately get in the way of our understanding of who we are. You may think you are a collection of experiences, such as traumas from your family that you never completely resolved, a mediocre high school education, and certain religious beliefs you once held closely but don't anymore. These offer, at best, only clues to your identity. But your identity is not formed by your experiences. It may be that, through your experiences, you can discover your identity, but your identity existed before you experienced anything.

Knowing our identity is enormously useful when we become advocates for our ideas. But long before the need for advocacy arises, identity serves as a check on whether what we are developing reflects the true us. Good people, holding good values, are unfortunately quite capable of creating things that are not inherently beneficial to others. Unintended consequences always occur and can undermine the best intentions. At least when we have made explicit who we are, we have a measure for whether our creations accurately reflect us. Knowing who we are also helps us see whether our work contributes to fulfilling what we are trying to do in the world.

The process of discovering one's true identity is not a simple one, and conveying the process in full lies beyond the scope of this book. But here are two hallmarks of real identity, which will help you know when you've discovered yours. First, identity brings unity to what has previously appeared to be an aggregate collection of passions and interests. When you know your identity, you will be able to see all these as expressions of one compelling drive. Second, when you know your identity, you will be clear about what it is you are driven to contribute to the world. Most of us walk around with a sense of great hunger, knowing we're capable of greatness but not sure how we're going to fulfill that yearning. When we finally get to our core, we validate that yearning and begin to fulfill its promise.

I have a question I put to clients who are struggling to get to their identity, and sometimes it can be helpful. In some ways it helps us to get out of ourselves and value the things about ourselves that are the beliefs we hold dearest — our sensitivity, our passion, our unique understanding.

Are you ready for the question? (Take a deep breath, and let it out.) If you were not successful in getting your way of seeing things out into the world, what is it the world would have lost?

Most of the authors I've worked with are eventually able to answer this question, and once they have, the answer guides their work, their book, the next book, and the rest of their lives.

What kinds of realizations about identity have driven some of the people I have worked with? I'll share a few: "I'm driven to help people understand that they need to listen to each other and really hear what the other person is trying to say. Then we can work together." "I have come to realize that I am not only living my life, but I also have the opportunity to use my life in a way of my choosing. I want people to understand that they can choose how to use their lives." "I am driven to help people understand that most of what they are told is simply not true, and that the only way they can ever know what is true is to see for themselves. They need to hold all their beliefs lightly and, when they realize something is closer to the truth, embrace it."

TRANSPARENCY

As I mentioned in the introduction, one of the obstacles to the speedy adoption of better ideas is that the potential user might focus on the person or people offering the solution, rather than on the solution itself. I was recently surveyed over the phone about my attitude toward home loan companies, and eventually the interview drilled down to how I felt about one high-profile company in particular, which was in the process of being merged into one of the major national banks. The purpose of the survey was to discover whether the name of the company that would be issuing a loan would affect my perception of the loan. Since the home loan company in this instance was going broke after creating billions of dollars in questionable loans to unsuspecting citizens, the answer was easy. I didn't trust the home loan company, and if the name were kept after the merger, I wouldn't sleep at night if my new loan had their name on the cover sheet. It's not just the money. It's also the identity, the soul, of the institution that counts. We do need to know who is the creator behind the curtain.

When we are developing something that we want

someone to want or buy or include in their thinking at some point in the future, it will be vastly easier for us to achieve success if we can remove ourselves from the conversation as quickly as possible. The best way to do that is to make who we are explicit to others right up front. This is who I am. This is who we are. This is what we stand for and what we believe we're up to.

I was speaking once with a group of business authors who were anxious to understand how to develop their authentic voice. I pointed out that almost all readers spend a fair amount of time, especially at the beginning of a book, trying to deconstruct the author and figure out what ax the author is grinding. Until readers are comfortable that they know who the author really is and what the author's intent is likely to be, readers can give only half their attention to the content. What is the ideal authentic voice? None! The author of ideas must disappear from the work, achieve transparency, and get out of the way of the content.

When you know your identity, not only do you know who you are and what you stand for, but you also know who and what you are not. Those who know their identity have no interest in being all things to all people. Instead they want to be themselves all the time, and be in relationship with others who are clear about who they are, so that highly productive relationships are possible.

For instance, if the passion and meaning of my life

is to discover the best possible way to teach young people, then others who might share my passion will easily recognize me for who I am, just as I will recognize them. With this recognition we can immediately benefit from the clarity of knowing who the other is. Then, no matter if some of them are architects devoted to schoolroom improvement, or educators devoted to the training of teachers, or designers of learning materials, or speech and language experts, we can all quickly exchange ideas and develop new and better ways to create learning environments for children.

In the development of powerful and authentic teams, there is no greater force than clarity around identity. If everyone on a team is driven to achieve goals in the world that are also coherent with the goals and drives of others in the team, and if that identity fits with the actual task at hand, the team will be capable of creating wonders.

Alignment of great forces often means that things can or will happen. Take the right ocean temperature, and align it with the right atmospheric pressure differences, and suddenly the great force of a hurricane can be unleashed. Organizations become agile when there is alignment between leadership, employees, goals, users, and products. In innovation, too, there is the possibility of an alignment between three forces that greatly enhances the possibility of success. The first force is the creator, the person or group that is driven to bring something new to the world. The second force is the creation itself. And the third force is the intended user. Only one of these identities is unchanging, and that is the identity of the creator, the one or ones doing the innovating. Knowing who you are will give you the necessary alignment guide throughout the creative process.

CHAPTER THREE

{ IMPLICATIONS }

The Reasonable Extremist

A genius thinker knows that
nothing exists in a moral vacuum.

This is the place for full divergence, where we follow all the possible rabbit trails. Where do our ideas lead? If what we are creating is valuable, then what are all the consequences we can imagine? Since we cannot know everything (all possible consequences good and bad, intended and not), we must be modest about what we think we know. But each alternative needs to be taken to every extreme imaginable, both positive and negative: while searching for success, we must also watch for all consequences.

THE BIGGEST PICTURE

One aspect of exploring implications is that the process eventually forces you into a complete worldview. If you accept a concept in isolation, without taking it to its extremes, the implications of the particular thing you are doing will never have the opportunity to bump up against all your other beliefs and values. Only by going to extremes do you force everything to become coherent — to get along intellectually, morally, ethically.

Almost no thing is without implications. Everything means something. So whenever we create something new, and we think through all the possible uses of what we are creating, we are likely to find some uses that violate our beliefs about what is right and wrong. At that point we must decide whether we have a moral obligation to address the possible wrong use of our innovation and determine whether that danger is worth the possible benefits. If we determine that going ahead is worthwhile, then we may want to do whatever we can to reduce the potential for our innovation to be used in ways that would do harm.

NOW IMPLICATIONS GO TO WORK

Not long ago pharmaceutical developers came up with a fairly effective cure for the common hangover. While it would be of immediate benefit to a great many people, the implication was that, if one of the behavior-shaping consequences of excessive drinking is a hangover, then removing this consequence might encourage alcohol abuse. This drug never came to market, since its introduction would have implied that excessive consumption of alcohol is acceptable.

The notion that we are responsible for the implications of everything we do will always keep us thinking about the big-picture possibilities of what we create, no matter what kind of innovation we engage in. If we are in the soft side of management, responsible for hiring, training, and managing people, we will want to examine carefully the underlying values we communicate in the training programs we develop. If we say to our trainees, "Every customer is important simply because each is a human being," the implication is that we as an organization also value our trainees simply because they deserve respect as human beings.

Imagine we are designing a new lightweight ladder and discover in our testing phase that it is possible, in maybe one out of a million instances, that, if someone is painting a house in a high wind, the ladder will develop a harmonic vibration and shake the painter off. We are now faced with making choices, all of them with implications. We can abandon the project altogether; we can continue with the ladder design unchanged and make sure our insurance is adequate to cover the occasional fallen painter; or we can continue our design development to reduce the effect of high winds on the ladder by design refinement through aeronautical testing. We can even put stickers all over the ladder warning that ladders are dangerous, so you're taking your life in your hands when you get on one; in the fine print we can list all the possible hazards of ladders in general and, in tiny tiny print, this design in particular.

There is a special aspect to almost all innovation in which we must look at possible misuse by those unable to fully protect themselves. Here I mean children and others without fully developed judgment. One of the fundamental implications for anyone introducing anything into the world is that all kinds of people might use it in ways we never intended. We don't want to find ourselves saying, "No one could have imagined that," when, in fact, we certainly could have and should have. In the early days of product-liability lawsuits, well-intentioned engineers of all kinds were shocked when something they had designed was used in a way they never intended, and injury, and even death, was the result. Little by little, good engineering has come to mean not only designing something to be used the way you want it to be used but also imagining all the possible misuses and doing everything possible to limit the damage from any of those misuses.

Sometimes, regardless of our best intentions, our creations can be so dangerously misused that, if we keep making them, the implication is that we don't care.

Look at the choice the 3M corporation had to make concerning the excellent spray glue they developed for mounting pictures. Artists and framers all over the world loved the product and came to depend on it. Unfortunately, a whole constituency of teenagers also came to depend on it for getting a special high that also caused liver damage. 3M could find no way to keep the spray glue from its unintended users, and so took the product off the market. The implication of that action was that they cared about the young people who would misuse their product more than they cared about the lost profit from its proper, intended use.

Let's look at the positive side of implications. A client of mine was working with one of the major power-generating utilities in the United States — let's call them Electrio — in an effort to help Electrio communicate better with their residential customers. In retreats and other team events, Electrio executives came to understand and believe that they stood for improving the quality of life in the home. They had in mind all those work-saving appliances they could power; the benefits of electric light, air-conditioning and filtering, and entertainment; as well as all the other wonders electricity brings us. With this new understanding, Electrio could communicate who they were and what they stood for with every bill, with every visit from a meter reader who might drop off an occasional seasonal reminder about how life in the home could be enhanced through new Christmas lights, or a new rotisserie on the barbeque, or even more efficient appliances.

The campaign went swimmingly for a year or so, until Electrio filed for permission to build a new coal-fired generating plant. Electrio's customers were concerned about air pollution and the potential contribution of the proposed plant to the problem of acid rain. Consumer groups began to use Electrio's understanding of the Electrio mission in questioning the wisdom of building the new plant. And interestingly, the people within Electrio began to wonder the same thing: If we stand for quality of life inside the home, maybe we shouldn't be building this new coal-fired plant, even though, in the short term, it is the least expensive way to generate electricity.

Eventually, Electrio decided on their own that the implications of building the new coal plant would undermine everything they believed they stood for, and announced, proudly, that they were going to invest in increased efficiency and renewable energy generation.

When we're creating something new, especially in technology, even small projects can have huge implications. The initial development of touch-sensitive screens was valuable for the development of ATMs, restaurant systems, and graphics applications. The art of the touch-screen interface stayed fairly unchanged even in the stylus-driven touch-screens of the Palm cell phones. When Apple decided to create a touch-screen interface for the iPhone, though, everything changed. First was the notion that certain hand behaviors could change the size of the screen. For the first time, the touch-screen was not just another version of a mouse interface. Here was an interface built for the hand. As Apple progressed in its development of the iPhone interface, it generated a regular flow of patents, since everything it was developing will have huge implications for all touch-screen interfaces of the future.

Returning to our toaster, let's assume that we've settled on making it a solar toaster. Imagine that we have come up with a light tube that allows us to put our solar gatherer anywhere near a kitchen window and have it transmit solar energy to the toaster, no matter where the toaster is in the customer's kitchen. When we make an innovation like that, we need to step back from our toaster work and take a little time to imagine all other possible uses for our remote solar-energy gatherer and transmitter. Where else might it be valuable? And once we've thought that through, we are likely to come up with all kinds of licensing opportunities, as well as develop a better understanding of how our solar-energy gatherer is going to work within the confines of our immediate challenge, the toaster. For instance, if one of our envisioned applications is a water heater or a baby bottle warmer, then highly accurate, reliable, yet inexpensive temperature control is going to be essential. So when we refine our little light valve that's going to govern temperature for the toaster, we will do it with an eye to its implications for other devices as well.

When we think something through while remaining sensitive to its implications, we are recognizing that nothing exists in a vacuum. Even the simplest idea, device, or strategy can affect the world in multiple ways. We need to see the moral, societal, and technological implications and play them out in every way imaginable to understand the full context of what we're doing.

To help us keep our projects' implications in mind, we might want to develop the habit of thinking about everything we're innovating as if each project were nitroglycerin, the powerful, unstable explosive. With nitro, we need to know exactly what makes it go off, and until we know what can stop it from exploding, we must handle it extremely carefully. Can a loud noise make it explode? Too much heat? Too much cold? Once we've figured this out, we can move on to the next step.

Taking this approach to our ideas helps us understand how far we can go with our new knowledge. As we work to develop an idea, we need to find out if we've reached the bedrock of what we're dealing with or are still dancing in the clouds. For any idea, the most visible implications are probably the ones that helped bring it to us in the first place. For instance, we might be trying to teach young children the basics of good behavior. We might discover that a story about squirrels helps them understand that good behavior means being aware of the feelings of others. The first implication we might draw from our discovery is that telling stories about animals is a terrific way to teach children empathic behavior. The next step we need to take is to discover whether in some circumstances stories about animals are no longer useful. We might discover, for example, that bullies don't care how little squirrels feel about other squirrels. In doing this testing, we'll be exploring the territory of our discoveries and seeking their limits, if any.

On the flip side of exploring every possible consequence of our discovery is that we must further torture ourselves by trying to imagine what the unintended consequences might be. Unintended consequences often result from failing to recognize the implications, either present ones or long-term ones, of our discovery. The negative side of the invention of the automobile, for example, is that it has destroyed the city, the countryside, and now almost the planet. Asbestos kept ships and buildings from burning, but it has killed tens of thousands of people. Television at first brought high culture into every home but eventually dumbed down the nation, as much of the populace became enfeebled by mindless entertainment. I am fascinated by the humbling power inherent in the possibility of unintended consequence. Knowing that we can't know all the side effects of what we are creating ought to prevent any but the most foolhardy from ever attempting anything too grandiose.

Fleshing out the implications of our ideas helps us to understand how far we can go with our new knowledge. Implications give us our landscape, the reach of our new domain.

CHAPTER FOUR

{ TESTING }

Find the Breaking Point

Genius thinkers know that the only way
to be certain something works is to discover
the test that would prove the opposite.

Testing means asking, "What am I blind to?" Asking yourself to see what you are not seeing is unlikely to give you the answer you need. That's why this is the time when you're going to need to put on your thickest skin and start showing carefully selected people what you're thinking about that you believe is new, original, and important.

At this point you must carefully avoid critics, naysayers, and devil's advocates. You are looking for appropriate early responders, for advocates. They are there to ask the right questions that help clarify your distinctions. Helpful advocates typically ask, "Did you mean X or Y?" Once they understand all the distinctions that may need to be sharpened, they will help you by thinking of implications and possible unintentional consequences.

An advocative early responder will always be asking you what your intentions are, directing their energy toward helping you communicate your work with as little ambiguity as possible. An advocate will not spend much time telling you what they think or arguing with you.

Think you've found a direct link between putting copper pennies in the ground and turning your hydrangeas blue? Say so, and send the idea around to a few friends in horticulture. Think you have the solution to making air travel delightful once again? Write it out and show it around. Want to compose the definitive memo on how to keep internal emails down to the absolute minimum? Write down your process in great detail and then send it to a few dozen really busy colleagues. You might generate some pretty interesting and helpful responses. (This will at least sort out those with a sense of humor.)

REPLICABILITY

Testing a concept often means determining whether or not it is replicable and whether others can teach it. We need to find out whether acceptance of the idea is dependent on its being associated with a particular charismatic individual, or whether it can stand on its own. This means that those who recognize the strength of their own personalities will need to be suspicious when judging the quality of their own ideas. There are a number of leading business consultants who are known for showing up and giving a humorous and brilliant hour-and-a-half keynote that gets everyone stirred up, yet when the dust clears, nothing will have changed. The fact that some people can charm an audience and have people hanging on their every word is not a test of the value of their distinctions. The true test is whether a person's ideas can in turn be presented by others who are trained to deliver them, or whether they can be transmitted via a book and get the same positive results.

Another test appropriate for ideas and methods intended to change a society over time is whether the new idea or system replicates and sustains its desired consequences over many generations. Religions and philosophies face this challenge, and deserve to be tested in this manner. We can ask: to what kind of civilizations and behaviors do these give rise? One would want to observe over a number of generations, and then take a look at what's being presented in the most recent generation and see how closely it follows the original intent.

This same test might fairly be applied to educational systems. Did the liberal arts curriculum that transformed the waves of immigrants before and during the Great Depression, and that gave way to the ad hoc process that educated the postwar baby boomers, do a better job of creating a self-sustaining educated populace than what followed? What about the Waldorf System, the Montessori System, or homeschooling?

What can you use to prove to yourself and others that what you have found to be true is self-replicable without your further intervention? Have someone else present your ideas, and see what gets transmitted. If you are the magic sauce of your ideas and they only flourish in your immediate presence, your thinking may not be sustainable yet and might need further development.

TEST FOR TRUTH

Ideas also need to be tested to see if they are true. If you can't find a test that would disprove your thinking, you will have a more difficult time improving it and sharing it. At the very least, you will be highly vulnerable to having someone besides yourself suddenly discover your idea's fatal flaw. The possibility of disproof would feel something like this: "If X is true, then what I am offering cannot be true." Your job is to look for those Xs. If I believe I have discovered a general truth that all animals are inherently kind to other animals, then the test is whether an example exists in which some animal, in nature, is cruel to another animal. One nasty monkey and my universal law will have to be modified. From then on I will need to say, "*Most* animals are inherently kind to one another."

How important is it to make these distinctions? They are the essence of thinking. Otherwise, we are blurring distinctions and failing to see or share what is true.

DESTRUCTIVE TESTING
TO FIND AND PUSH LIMITS

The point of destructive testing is not to destroy but to find the weakness in a complex system, such as a bridge or a machine. When we're destructive-testing something, we're looking carefully for the first sign of failure. We might even choose to stop our testing at the first crack in the metal, strengthen that part, and then see what starts to fail next.

Imagine trying to build a better car door. Once we have our new prototype, we need to build a machine that can slam and open that door a million times. As the number of slams climbs into the thousands, all kinds of little failures will show up — wear on the hinges, a groove in the strike plate, a sticky linchpin. The window may start to rattle. Screws will fall out of the door panel. If we wanted to, we could continue to slam and strengthen and reengineer the door and all its parts until our door could survive millions of slams without a failure of any kind.

If we're engineering a device, whether it's aircraft landing gear, an artificial heart, or a rubberband-driven glider, at some appropriate point in destructive testing we can call a halt and accept the design. You might wonder why we would accept any kind of failure. And the only logical answer is that failure is certain. The question has to be: what length of mechanical life is acceptable?

The implication for nonmechanical systems, such as a treatment protocol for a disease, or computer software, is that there will always be shortcomings. A medical protocol — a generally accepted best way of doing something — always compromises with the perfect, but patients are sick and doctors need to act. A computer operating system will always become obsolete. When testing our system, we will always reach a point when we must decide that, even though it's not perfect, it's good enough to provide value. We can put our discoveries and innovations to work and then, if necessary, either now or in the future, begin our task of further refinement.

TEST AGAINST INTENTION

In softer systems, too, destructive testing is necessary. Organization design, whether corporate or governmental, rarely turns out to be perfect at the first iteration. Even if we get everything right the first time, circumstances change over time. Whether we want it to be or not, we can think of time itself as being a natural destructive test. Therefore, we need to build in systems and people whose job it is to look for the first signs of time-caused failures in all our systems so we can fix them before catastrophic failure occurs and we crash.

Just as we could find endless refinement through destructive testing, we must test our creations against our original intent, need, and vision, make careful note of our shortfalls, and refine our work. Imagine we're building a teaching system to teach first graders to read, a system based on a breakthrough understanding of how children's brains get wired for verbal skills. We create new reading materials, teacher's manuals, visual aids, and parent communication. Then we take it out and try it on some actual children. We observe, take careful notes, and then refine and refine. The better our observation skills, the better our interview skills, the faster we can refine our ideas as we get closer to our original intent. But, of course, all the refinement in the world will not make our new system a success unless our methodology was solid in the first place.

We can think of the Founding Fathers' plan for the United States as expressed in the Constitution as a grand piece of organizational design, and the process of the past 220-plus years as being destructive testing of their original premises. Can a system of checks and balances stay balanced? Will a democracy inherently educate its children so that the electorate will be capable of making enlightened decisions? Is market capitalism compatible with the desire to create a society that benefits the common good?

VINTAGE

One of my clients is a California winemaker and a restless innovator. In working with him, I discovered a new understanding of how time can be the limiting factor in one's testing. Imagine you are trying new grapes in new soil and a new climate to see how well they work together. Imagine you are blending some of those grapes with grapes from other locales. Some of the wine, you put in French oak barrels for six months. Another portion of it goes straight into stainless steel. At one year, you blend it all back together and get an early sense of how the aging is going. In two or three years you taste again. In twenty-five years you taste again. Most wineries accumulate a "library," a collection that the winemaker can taste over the years in order to learn from variations of grape and *terroir*, adjusting for the climate of a given year and other variations in the vintage. Humbling to think about, isn't it? When my client said to me, "A winemaker has only so many vintages in his life," it made clear to me how fortunate most of us are to be able to test in cycles of a few weeks or months.

THE FIRST ADVOCACY HOOKS EMERGE

During the process of testing, we will have the opportunity to observe and hear about successes along the way. It will be extremely valuable for us to become curators of those successes as we go, since they will fuel the final step, the eleventh step of the Endleofon — advocacy. All the genius innovation and creativity in the world means nothing if we cannot find a way to accelerate the acceptance of what we have created. If, in our early-stage testing of our new fabric cleaning solution, we hear someone say, "That stain has been there since my grandmother owned it, and suddenly, it's gone," that remark's a keeper, an *advocacy hook*. If a child suddenly says, "I love reading this way," we know we have a quote that will help us interest others.

MODELING

Models, analogues to what we are creating, can greatly shorten testing time and reduce its cost. I don't understand why every single organization doesn't have a model of itself in which scenarios of all kinds can be tested without doing damage to the actual organization. When I first moved to publishing from filmmaking in the early days of the personal computer, in order to understand how publishing worked from a financial perspective I built as complete a model as I could of the life of a book, taking into consideration the hardcover and paperback editions, foreign rights sales, the number of words (therefore pages), manufacturing cost per word (and therefore per page), cover design, author's advance, and so on. My model also took time into consideration, since a book's life, from initial proposal to pulping of the last remaindered copy, can take several years.

I began to play with my model, showing it to experienced publishing hands of all kinds, asking them to find flaws in it and to help me refine it. Not a lot of people in publishing were using PCs at the time, and many were skeptical that a book could be modeled. But here's the great thing about financial models — they just get better over time. The more you look at the real world of your organization, and then check the model against it and refine the model, the more powerful your tool will be at predicting the effect of anything and everything you can do to your organization.

At the time I made my first publishing model, in the late 1980s, paper costs were rapidly on the rise. When I plugged in the numbers for what were called "category" books, which meant paperback romances, science fiction, military adventure, and westerns, I realized that this type of book could never turn a profit if the length was more than 192 pages, no matter what. The model was useful for guiding everyone in the organization to an understanding of the limit of what we could spend on marketing, and of the break-even point, for every book. We began to see that every title was, in effect, its own little business with its own profit-and-loss statement.

We can also make physical models for our projects, when that is appropriate. Wilbur and Orville Wright built a rectangle-shaped open-ended wind tunnel out of a wooden box. It was sixteen inches wide by sixteen inches tall by six feet long. Inside of it they placed an aerodynamic measuring device made from an old hacksaw blade and bicycle-spoke wire. Over a two-month period they tested more than two hundred models of different types of wings.

Octave Chanute, a close collaborator of the Wrights, was in frequent correspondence with them as the wind tunnel experiments continued. Within a month of completing the tunnel, Chanute wrote to Wilbur Wright, "It is perfectly marvelous to me how quickly you get results with your testing machine. . . . You are evidently better equipped to test the endless variety of curved surfaces than anybody has ever been."

On January 10, 1902, Wilbur Wright wrote to Chanute, "I think our experiments show conclusively that man can build wings far superior to those of any bird in efficiency in soaring." *

---

* Marvin W. McFarland, ed., *The Papers of Wilbur and Orville Wright* (New York: McGraw-Hill, 2000).

On December 17, 1903, the Wright Brothers took humankind aloft in powered flight for the first time.

My favorite story about the creation of a brilliant analogue comes from the BBC, and takes place shortly after World War II, at a time when the great broadcasting system was the leading developer of sound-recording technology. The BBC was building a new broadcast studio, and the leading engineers and acousticians had a pretty good idea, based on measurements taken in favorite halls around the world, of the decay times (very long decay times are known as echo) they would like to have in their new studio. They also knew which frequencies they wanted to decay faster, which slower, and other complex ideals for mixing of the sound while maintaining clarity. Acoustics, then as now, was often considered a black art, and plans developed by the greatest acoustic geniuses often resulted in miserable performance spaces.

In those days, the BBC was on a tight budget, so the team decided to model the acoustics of the studio they were about to build. Now, sound travels at something more than 760 miles per hour through air. How can you build a miniature space that will allow you to model the behavior of sound? The engineers built a one-eighth model of the proposed studio, installed tiny speakers and microphones, and multiplied the frequencies they were observing by eight. After months of refining — changing the shape of the side walls and the ceiling height, and playing with the right mixture of absorptive and reflective materials — they had a model with the properties they wanted.

The actual studio was eventually constructed, and its acoustics measured almost exactly as the model had predicted.

Modeling also has the potential to make the obscure clear. Francis Crick and James Watson had a pretty good understanding of the chemical components of DNA. What they couldn't get right was the molecular structure, and without that, DNA remained a beguiling but abstract concept. When, with their Tinkertoy-like modeling components, they were able to construct the famous double-helix shape, they could suddenly see for the first time how DNA worked. As soon as they were able to build a model that satisfied everything they knew about DNA, they immediately knew they had unlocked its secrets and that they had secured for themselves the Nobel Prize.

THE METAPHOR TRAP

The models we have just been looking at reflect the idea of analogue as the Greeks first used it, where the ratios of one thing are the same as the ratios of another. True analogues can tell us a great deal if we choose them well. The small can stand for the large, as the Wright brothers' wing models in their modest wind tunnel did for the final wings that took Orville aloft at Kitty Hawk, or as the wiggles in a vinyl record groove are an analogue to the rapid changes in air pressure that we interpret as sound. In these instances, the ratios really are the same.

Metaphors and similes, figures of speech that point up the resemblance of one thing to another, can often appear to provide the same insights as do analogues. We can declare the challenges of building and running our company at the same time is "flying a 747 while we're building it." That metaphor conveys the feeling we might have about the difficulty of our task at hand, but if we try to use the metaphor in the same way that we can use a true analogy, we will be wandering into a metaphor trap. If we draw from the 747 metaphor that we'd better carry a full load of fuel since we don't know when the landing gear will be ready, there might be a tiny bit of insight there. But if we try to figure out how fast we ought to fly, or at what altitude, and what the meaning of pressurization is, the metaphor will be, at best, not valuable and, at worst, completely misleading.

There is no question that people love metaphors. They're colorful, and they can connect all kinds of situations that might be difficult to grasp to those that are much easier to grasp. Complicated business strategies are often described as sport. Desperate gambles can be justified momentarily as "going deep." Old, loyal employees can be fired if we think of them as "retreads." The danger of metaphors is that they have the ring of truth without passing any test of truth. And if we take the metaphor further and begin to make decisions based on it, we will be falling into the metaphor trap. If we really think we're in a baseball game and it's the last game of the World Series, and we're down by one run, then we might take out our starter (our CEO) and bring in an ace from the bench to save the game and the series. The flaw is that the baseball season is finite, and there is a World Series every year. Our business does not go down to the last hour on an annual basis. We might need our CEO tomorrow.

When John Sculley was taking over Apple and forcing Steve Jobs out, the operating metaphor on the Sculley side was: "What's the difference between Apple and the Boy Scouts? One of them has adult leadership!" So the metaphor tells us that Apple resembles the Boy Scouts. It also tells us that Steve Jobs is not an adult. If the metaphor was true, then Steve Jobs clearly needed to go. You can see how dangerous a metaphor like that can be if the board of directors accepts it as being true. The reality is that whatever the "problem" concerning Steve Jobs was, that problem was not adequately captured by metaphorically calling him a nonadult. The metaphor trap blinded the Apple board to the real issues and a wise solution.

THE MIRACLE OF ANALOGUE

Analogues make terrific dashboards, both in our cars and in our planes. Your analogue fuel gauge, speed-ometer, tachometer, and temperature gauge give you instant and meaningful accurate ratios that tell you if your speed is thirty or sixty, if your tank is half or three-quarters full, and if your engine is right in the middle of the operating temperature range where it's supposed to be. If you had all digital gauges, you would need to translate each number. If your fuel gauge reads 2.1, you'd need to translate this to miles per gallon, or calculate the tank capacity, to get a feeling for when you need to refuel.

Testing, including modeling, is the only reliable way we have of finding out how robust our ideas are. With-out the appropriate test, whatever we are developing may hide its weaknesses and will remain suspect, vul-nerable, unimproved. With the right tests, ideas become rigorous.

CHAPTER FIVE

{ PRECEDENT }

The Great Conversation

Genius thinkers know
they are standing on the shoulders of others.

Although genius thinkers are confident in their own unique ability to innovate, they understand that they will benefit from the previous work of others, regardless of when that thinking took place.

As soon as we begin to have a pretty good grasp of our idea, it's time to ask, "Who else has seen something like this?" Robert Hutchins, who cofounded, with Mortimer Adler, the Great Books of the Western

World program for Encyclopedia Britannica, saw the process of human wisdom as a restless dialogue that humanity is engaged in that stretches back through the centuries to the beginning of human thought. Hutchins called this dialogue the Great Conversation. By recognizing that we are creating something of value, we are automatically entering into that Great Conversation.

By being aware of the Great Conversation, we can search for similar solutions to the challenge we are facing, and we might even discover models of success that would be useful. Ideally, we would be able to search the world's knowledge base and be able to learn every positive and cautionary bit possible from that knowledge. And we must search for concurrent knowledge, as well.

Here we come across the nub of what is so humbling about presuming to create anything new. In order not to reinvent the wheel, it is worthwhile to know what has already been thought or said by those who came before us, and by our contemporaries. It would not be unintelligent of us to assume that someone, somewhere, has already thought about what we're trying to do, and maybe in a better way. And yet . . . in spite of the possibility that someone has already said, somewhere, much of what I have to say, I am writing this book, and I believe that if you read it, it will help you be brilliant in your thinking.

Why should you pursue this folly of trying to put together your ideas when you are faced with the undercutting idea that you may never really know whether or not your thoughts are original? As you develop your thinking, it is probably wise to assume someone, somewhere, has already articulated at least a few elements of what you have to say. Yet it may be just as safe to assume that no one has put together what you are working on in such a way that they have reached the same complete understanding that you have.

As we develop as human beings, it is normal for us to assume that everyone is pretty much the same as we are. When we are young, if a certain kind of music goes right to our heart, we assume our friends feel the same way. If at age seven we are enormously empathetic with the hurts of one of our friends, we assume that others around us are similarly sensitive to the sufferings of others. I have come to believe that, for some of the most important aspects of ourselves, for the things that are most unique about our understanding of the world, the opposite may be true. It may be that the things we know or feel deeply, that immutable part of us we feel we were born with, make up the most importantly unique aspect of ourselves. These special ways of feeling and sensing and intuiting are the oceans we swim in. You may have heard the observation that fish have no understanding of water — that they have no awareness of water since it is their universal and constant. We are our own water:

our true self is the thing we are least likely to see or to perceive as being unusual. And yet, being able to distinguish this true self would be our most precious knowledge, if only we could see it clearly.

In the early days of thinking through what would become his two major statements on identity, *Identity Is Destiny* and *The Identity Code*, Larry Ackerman tried to explain to me the importance of the concept that organizations have identity just as people do. I wasn't quite getting it. Larry suddenly exclaimed: "Don't you see — if organizations have an identity, then the laws of identity would apply to them, too." Larry was assuming that his most fundamental beliefs were obvious to everyone, in fact so obvious that they didn't even need to be stated. He was at the brink of seeing, for the first time, the ocean he was swimming in, by making the important distinction that this knowledge was unique to him. I asked Larry what the laws of identity were. At that moment he was only able to state two. Over the next six months or so, he discovered the rest of the laws of identity deep in his consciousness and has not stopped thinking and writing about their implications and inspiring others with his knowledge ever since. The one thing he assumed everyone knew, because it was so important and fundamental to the way he saw the world, turned out to be the core of what was unique to himself.

How can you get out of your own ocean to see what differentiates you? One way is to be aware that you are inexorably entering a conversation when you think about something. Search, read, and discover what others have said or are saying. Then begin to be specific about what you see in the same ideas, and note whether or not there are distinctions between what you see and what has already been said. In noticing the kinds of distinctions you tend to make, you will discover your gifts, your values, and your passions. You will realize that you have a way of seeing things, and that your way is like no one else's. I am going to take a little leap here on this: I think that when anyone is able to know themselves in this way, to know how they are different and how they uniquely see the world, then they are ready to make their contribution. What is the potential of one person's contribution? I believe that in every human being is the potential to illuminate the nature of human existence for all of us. All anyone needs to do is tell us what they know.

These conversations we enter when we are making new distinctions can span centuries. It's as if we're perpetually walking into a meeting late, not knowing who has already said what. If we speak without getting a grasp of what's already been said, we'll risk appearing like an idiot. The hard fact is, when it comes to the conversation of ideas, we will always be coming into the meeting late. So we must do the best we can to catch up, to find out what's already been said. Then we can bring our ideas to light in an informed context.

Knowing what has been said will help us refine our own ideas and find a shared language. The notion that we need to put our ideas out there, without having perfect knowledge of the conversation we are entering, explains the essential risk that's involved with saying anything. We can't have perfect knowledge. But we also can't make our fear of appearing foolish prevent us from saying or developing what we see. We must make a reasonable effort to discern the originality and value of our discovery; and once we've done so, it's appropriate to take the risk and be heard.

As part of our research to discover where we are in the conversation, we should find out upon whose shoulders we are standing, since knowing where we fit in the evolution of our ideas will be useful to us and our audience. It is okay to acknowledge the people whose thinking inspired us. When I started out to write this book, I considered myself to be standing on the shoulders of a few writers whose books had influenced me as an English student in high school. I turned back to one of these books to take a fresh look at what had once been so useful to me. I rediscovered a sentence in William Zinsser's *On Writing Well* that long ago had struck a chord in me, and that has since evolved into a way of life. "It is impossible for a muddy thinker to write good English." Returning to that sentence for the first time in many decades, I was both thrilled to see it and struck that Zinsser had quickly moved on from that sentence to return to the theme of his chapter, which was the need for simplicity for the reader's sake. Left for others to work on was the notion of what constitutes muddy thinking and what might help us begin to think clearly.

Authors who have absorbed the thinking of others should not be overly concerned about being accused of not being original. Once you have absorbed your major influences, everything you think and do will tend to be original, because only you can synthesize them in the unique way that you do.

By taking the chance of expressing what we have discerned, we take the inherent risk that we have missed something, and also that what we have to say has already been said. With a reasonable amount of research, we can discover where our original thinking fits in, and having done so, we can begin to make our unique contribution to the great river of human thought.

Some years ago a business partner and I were introducing a British high-end bookshelf loudspeaker to the U.S. market. Instead of just sending the speakers out with sales reps and hoping for the best, we embarked on a rather ambitious journey, making a continuous automobile tour to all the high-end audio stores in the United States. When we arrived at one of these stores, we would set up a head-to-head match between our speakers and whatever the store considered its best for anywhere near the same price. Within a few months we had compiled a rather complete view of the high-end market in the United States and established a complete dealer network for our speakers. We then made our first visit to the Consumer Electronics Show, where we strolled from booth to booth, hotel room to hotel room, listening to the hundreds of new speaker systems that were being introduced that year, the vast majority of which would never make it to market. Some were decent, most were simply mediocre. But without exception, all were designed by engineers enthralled by their own breakthroughs.

As my partner tried to figure out why so many hundreds of people would be clueless about the quality and significance of what they had created, he observed that each of these engineers had been so focused on improving his own creation, and proving its underlying theory, that the engineer had simply not done the work of looking around to see what else was already out there.

The lesson of this is quite simple. It's not that every speaker designer needed to listen to each one of the thousands of speakers that might be competitive. All they needed to do was listen to the three or four generally accepted best speakers in the world at that moment to see how their own work compared. Without knowing the current state of the art, they could not know what their starting point needed to be.

How does this work for whatever we might be developing? We don't need to know everyone who is developing something in our field. All we need to do is find out who is doing the best work and see how what we are doing compares to that. Whether it's our solar toaster, or our reading program for first graders, or our plan for universal health care, all we need to do, to join the conversation at its highest level, is find the best.

This helps us solve the challenge that at first seems so intimidating: if the conversation we're joining really began at the beginning of human thought, how can we ever know everything? And the answer is, fortunately, we don't need to. All we have to do is seek out the best in our precedents and ignore the rest.

How Do We Find the Best?

Ask as many people as you can who are knowledgeable in the area you're working in to tell you what they think is the current state of the art in your field. If you're working in a field that has a huge history, as do most design fields (like architecture) and most of the arts (like poetry or theater) the same applies. You needn't hesitate to write a poem just because you haven't yet read all the greats, yet as you explore your creativity you will also want to catch up on the conversation you're entering. Once you're writing or designing, you'll find that your ability to look closely at others' work, even if across many centuries, will be greatly enhanced. Spend a few afternoons trying to get a pastel of a sky to look the way you want it to, and the next time you look at a Turner you'll have a whole new understanding.

If you're working in the sciences or technology, then being current takes a lot of effort, because valuable new work takes place continually across the planet. You will need to discover the best filters in your area, and use them.

What are filters? Filters are those people who look at everything that might be of interest to their intended audience and select what they think is valuable. The editors of the *New York Times*, for example, filter the world's events, sorting out from thousands of stories those that they think anyone who wants to stay current will need to know. Since their intended audience is several million people, their sieve isn't very fine.

For every specialty in science, the arts, technology, management, and political science, there are also filters in print and online. As you begin to discover various potential audiences for what you are developing, you may want to find the filters your intended audience is using so that you can join in their conversations within their context.

For instance, let's imagine we are developing a tracking system and database that will help manufacturers, warehouses, and retailers track the location of thousands of individual items. In our exploration to discover who else might find our technology valuable, we realize that librarians might benefit from being able to easily tag hundreds of thousands of books, magazines, and journals and track them with our new system. But before we approach the library market, it would be worthwhile to find the librarians' preferred filter to see what's on the typical librarian's mind and the language currently used to address libraries' challenges.

Another reason to examine the great conversation, even as far back as we can, is that old technologies, old ideas, old designs, and old concepts can help us, inspire us, and give us a richer sense of the context we're working in. A screenwriter working on a science fiction script might find inspiration in Aeschylus and decide that the crew of his spaceship can function as an ancient Greek chorus from time to time. Even engineers can be inspired by ancient work, as well as by developments that took place when a now "obsolete" technology was first developed. Vacuum tubes were long ago replaced by the discrete transistor and eventually the integrated circuit, yet vacuum tubes and their early circuits have been revived in high-end audio applications. As we seek to reduce our carbon impact, we might look again at earlier forms of refrigeration, such as caves. When we think about lighting our interiors and consider reducing our electrical consumption, we might look again at buildings designed before electricity and see what a thousand years of experience in designing with natural light came up with. The great British architect

Christopher Wren, who died in 1723, comes to mind. His Saint Paul's cathedral, on even the cloudiest day in London, requires no additional electric light.

Is It an Improvement?

Joining the Great Conversation can save us a lot of time and grief by letting us see the blind alleys and lost trails of others who have worked in our area. And let's not get distracted by the metaphor trap of "not reinventing the wheel." In reality, the wheel gets reinvented all the time because we need an almost infinite variety of wheels. The gear was a reinvention of the wheel, as was the pneumatic tire. Nano wheels are being invented that will make nano machines, coming soon to an artery near you.

Shuffling the Deck

Genius thinking means taking your new ideas and testing them against old failures to see if what you've discovered unblocks someone else's long-ago discarded area of development. Breakthroughs of all kinds mean that we need to look backward as well as forward, and to think about things that couldn't have been done at some time in the past because there were simply too many obstacles, but which are now within our grasp. What if, in the process of developing our solar toaster, we discover a way to capture solar heat and move it anywhere we want? Our breakthrough would affect heating and air-conditioning designs, cooking systems, and architecture. I like to think of big breakthroughs as shuffling the deck, completely changing the hand we've been dealt. The personal computer shuffled the deck, as did the Internet. In whatever field we're in, we need to be highly alert to shuffle-the-deck breakthroughs and willing to reexamine everything we know, since, in many ways, everything will now change.

Geniuses always have their antennas out for shuffle-the-deck breakthroughs in their own immediate area and in the world in general. This is one reason why we need to develop our own personal array of filters that will bring us the information we need as soon as it happens. Shuffle-the-deck breakthroughs in the Great Conversation change the conversation.

ZEITGEIST

When we join the Great Conversation, we are often moving into other time periods, epochs, eras, cultures. Some of us wonder what it would be like to have lived during the Renaissance in Italy or fought in the U.S. Civil War. When we use that strange pairing of the words *be like*, we usually mean: what were the intangibles that gave the period its flavor? When we become sensitive to the spirit of the time, or zeitgeist, we become increasingly sensitive to the spirit of the moment of our own time. If you were to step back from the period we're living in right now, how would you capture the essence of it so that someone reading your thoughts fifty years from now could catch the subtle flavor of this moment?

Understanding the flow of the zeitgeist, being sensitive to it, will help us calibrate our own innovations and developments. Certain ideas and projects may run heavily against the spirit of the time, which will greatly increase the difficulty of their introduction and acceptance. When we understand the zeitgeist, we can attempt to shape our developments so that they flow with it. For instance, if in publishing at the moment there is great enthusiasm for memoirs, a story of how our innovations transformed our organization might find greater acceptance if told as our personal story of growth and discovery. If the zeitgeist is running heavily against energy-consuming appliances, then our solar toaster might find rapid acceptance if marketed as an anti-appliance.

When someone says, "What's working these days is...," what they're talking about is the zeitgeist, and if they really know something, then it's worthwhile to pay attention.

There is a mysteriously strong bent in a number of people and cultures to believe that the world they are in at the moment is unique, and that ideas and solutions must be developed from whole cloth in order to address that current unique situation. We see these blinders at work as we seek solutions in national policy issues, where we barely take a moment to look at solutions that might be working just fine elsewhere. It's a shame, since discovering the right precedent can be a great help to us, with the potential to give us a slingshot forward.

CHAPTER SIX

{ NEED }

We Are Not Alone

Genius thinkers recognize that,
when they have created something of value
in any one area, it will probably be of value
in many areas.

L et's imagine we've just developed a complete pneumatic tube system for our large pharmaceutical manufacturing campus. (Pneumatics were popular in the nineteenth century, with narrowbore tubes that carried mail under the streets of Paris and the first demonstration subway in New York both running on pneumatic principles: if you fit a cylinder into a tube of a slightly greater diameter, you can propel the cylinder at high speed using only air pressure.) Imagine that we're able to take materials, even delicate ones, and send them several miles around our campus in a few seconds. To develop this system, we have reengineered those nineteenth-century pneumatics, and we also have new, self-switching thermally stable capsules, clear pneumatic tubing, switches, and bulletproof logic, so that no matter what the failure, nothing can ever be damaged.

Now that we've got this system up and running, we can begin to ask who else might benefit from all of our innovations. The first possibility is: No one! It could just be that something we have seen or created for ourselves has an audience or interest group of one. Part of the essence of identity is that we are unique, and therefore there is some likelihood that, even though something we have created absolutely drives us wild with joy, we are completely alone in this appreciation. This goes for authors, inventors, composers, and other innovators of all kinds. It can be quite a challenge to find that what pleases us so much has no other takers. When the whole world says no to you, it can be a lot of rejection to handle, unless you can accept it as a recognition of you as an individual. Undoubtedly, other creations of yours will find acceptance, especially if they are created with the identity of users other than yourself in mind.

As a pharmaceutical manufacturer, we can make a reasonable assumption that we are not, in fact, alone. So we certainly have potential customers for our pneumatic system in other pharmaceutical manufacturers.

We can also imagine all kinds of other manufacturers who might benefit from the just-in-time capabilities of our pneumatics. If we really want to expand our vision, we could imagine convincing UPS to replace their entire truck parcel delivery system with a national system of larger bore pneumatics delivering everything from books to food. Imagine if the speed of ordering over the Internet could almost be matched by delivery speed. One click on Amazon and your book slips into a capsule and heads through the network at a thousand miles an hour to your office or residence drop box.

As we solve our local problems and innovate for our own organizations, or even just for ourselves, we need to ask, who else needs this knowledge? If what I am saying is so, for whom would this knowledge be valuable? This question forces us out of focusing solely in our own area and may even lead us to find new universals that underlie our work. Having a good understanding of who needs us most will also help us in crafting our development, because we will want to be useful to as wide an audience as we might ultimately want to attract.

When we think about those potential secondary users, we have a number of choices to make. If our core work is pharmaceutical development, do we really want to be distracted by going into the pneumatics business? So for those others who might also benefit from our discoveries, we could consider giving the information away, or licensing it to someone else to continue its development, or even spinning off a new company to pursue the business. We also need to ask ourselves essential competitive questions. Should we share our innovations with our entire industry? Or should we keep our knowledge secret and exploit it as long as we can as a competitive advantage? To this day, across the globe, there are only a few people who are allowed to see the machines that transform polystyrene into coffee cups, ensuring the continued billions in profits for Dart Industries.

WHO WILL IT BE MOST VALUABLE FOR?

If you have discovered something of value, chances are it will be of value for a far larger audience than the one you initially created it for. Sometimes, once you recognize your largest possible audience, you will continue the work with the larger audience or market in mind, and your thinking will broaden and the value you bring will be increased.

For instance, if you have discovered the secret of how to motivate seven-year-olds, you might think your core audience is the parents of seven-year-olds. But you will soon discover that teachers of seven-year-olds will also be interested. And chances are that some of what you have to say, although developed from your acute observations of seven-year-olds, might also be useful for motivating eight-year-olds and six-year-olds. Often we start out looking at a narrow base because we have made our discoveries while addressing our own specific problems. When we begin to think about our audience, we want to step back and ask who else would benefit from the underlying ideas that we have developed.

Maybe you are a hospital color consultant and have discovered that certain colors bring about shorter labor in women giving birth, other colors raise performance in the operating theater, and still others speed recovery in intensive care. As valuable as this knowledge will be for those designing and managing hospitals, it might also have value for architects of all kinds, designers, psychologists, educators, and families.

Sometimes knowing that you might also have an audience outside the area in which you first made your discovery will cause you to broaden your thinking. Use the Endleofon steps 4, Testing, and 8, Completion, to help you determine how great a span your work might cover. Obviously, there are limits to how thin you might be able to stretch your developments without risking appearing foolish, yet exploring who else would benefit will help you settle on who your imagined users are. Once you have chosen your target users, you will be able to refine your work for them. And because you know who they are and how urgently they will want the knowledge you are trying to give them, you will be more likely to bring your work to a practical level so it can be quickly grasped and put to use.

Imagine you are developing a powerful therapeutic technique that addresses troubled adult relationships at risk of falling apart. Your work will be valuable for therapists and for couples who are currently getting along but who may have had some bumpy spots in the past. But your core users, the people who most urgently need what you have to say, are those who are in the midst of a struggle to maintain their relationships' integrity. When you complete your work with them in mind, you will feel this urgency. And when they see your process, they will look at it in a way that is completely different from the way everyone else will look at it. Think about your neediest users as you develop your work, and focus on them. All other interested users will sense the urgency inherent in that first-priority relationship and will closely watch for positive outcomes.

CHAPTER SEVEN

{ FOUNDATION }

Discover the House Rules

When working with something new,
a genius thinker steps back from time to time and asks:
What are the underlying principles operating here?
Or are we using new rules, and if so, can they be pulled
together into a coherent group or body of law?

Everything we think is true either is a fundamental principle or relies on one. Some groups of fundamental principles can be gathered together into what we think of as a body of law. The first may have been the Code of Hammurabi, followed by the Ten Commandments and, in more recent times, Newton's laws of motion, Maslow's hierarchy of needs, Ackerman's laws of identity, and even Bill Smith's Six Sigma. Each of these bodies of law is an attempt to give us complete guidelines in the area it addresses. Knowing that we have the complete body makes it vastly easier to live our lives and even to be creative.

The search for rules is really about navigation. If we are embarking on a new project, or thinking about something completely new, it can feel as if we're going to sea with nothing but a tiny boat, a little sail, and a couple of sandwiches. There are three types of bodies of law that can operate here — and we need to know which one applies to any given project we work on. First, we might be in a world of real, preexisting rules. All we need to do is be aware that we are in such a world and find out what those rules are. The second possibility is that we are working within a group of laws or principles that we intuit may exist but that have not yet surfaced. And finally there are rules or laws that we make up because we need to put some boundaries around our innovative work.

Let's take a look at how those three frameworks might operate. If we're working in the framework of given laws, our task of discovering our framework is much easier: we're working within the laws set down by our government, or the laws of nature, or the laws of our organization. All we need to do is know what the laws are and we can work within them.

Finding our assumed laws is more difficult, because we will need to dig them out. The great reward here, though, is that, if we can indeed discover those assumed laws, articulating them will be helpful to ourselves and possibly to a great many other people. For instance, if we can discover the six laws of winning any argument, or the twenty-two laws of a successful wedding, or the one law of human happiness, then we're on the edge of making a real contribution to the world's knowledge.

Imagine you are an engineer whose job is to design a steel bridge that's going to carry freight trains over a chasm. If you knew some of the rules that apply to your work, such as the necessity for testing the soils for foundation requirements, requirements for grounding steel structures, and momentum formulas that must be used for determining your span length, but couldn't be assured that you knew all of the rules, it would be very difficult, if not impossible, to design your bridge with confidence that your creation, once built, would serve safely over its entire expected lifetime. But if you knew that everything you needed to consider was within that single *Rules for Building Steel Bridges* volume that's sitting on your desk, you could proceed with great efficiency.

Finally, for the instance of when we might need to simply make our laws up, think about that solar toaster. What if someone in our group has the brilliant idea that the most efficient way to make it work is to launch a satellite that will beam infrared energy to all subscribers to our toaster energy system? There's nothing wrong with our team agreeing, at that point, that any solution involving launching a new kind of satellite is off the table.

Finding which framework we're operating in will help speed our development process, and later, when we make our principles clear to others, we will be speeding the adoption of what we've created.

HOW TO SURFACE HIDDEN PRINCIPLES

Almost everything we say or do has significance and carries implications. When we are developing something, it becomes especially important to be able to decode ourselves in order to see our own underlying beliefs clearly and to eventually make clear the relationship of our principal underlying beliefs to each other.

We can often discover our entire framework by looking closely at any single element of what we're creating, since the truth of the whole is carried in every one of its parts. Everything we create, in each of its parts, expresses our values, our expression of what we think is the nature of life and humankind, our hopes for ourselves and the world.

THE WHY PROCESS

Most statements carry an implied worldview, deeply hidden under some camouflage. So that we can eventually try to integrate our values into a coherent whole, we will want to practice a methodology widely used by curious children.

Ever try to explain to a child why water is wet, or why the sky is blue, or where thunder comes from? To any answer, a persistent child, if not yet thoroughly satisfied, will just keep asking "Why?" until they get to the root of the matter (if the parent doesn't strangle the child along the way). We, too, can take this naïve yet powerful path, asking "Why?" and "Why?" again until we drill down to some kind of truth. And maybe not just any truth, but the Truth. Because at the end of all those "Whys?" is the big "Because." "Because God made it that way," or "Because there is no God," or "Because there may or may not be a god, but we'll all be better off if we act as if there is a God."

I believe that until we find an answer for ourselves to the big "Why?" that we can live with for a while, we will not be able to think through the moral implications of our personal universe. And not having thought through an answer to that "Why?," we will have difficulty thinking clearly. I know this might seem like an enormous leap, but not knowing our beliefs about how the world works puts us on a shaky platform from which to make our observations. When we think about how people might best learn, or how we ought to treat others, or plan our lives, our thoughts need to be in the context of what we believe to be true about the nature of human existence.

This simplistic-seeming exercise of asking "Why?" and then "Why?" again to each answer that follows, will take us to the root of what we're really saying, almost all the time. Of course, it is extremely difficult to ask ourselves "Why?" at every turn, and yet if we hope to achieve clear thinking, we must do this for ourselves or have someone take us through the "Why?" process. You might consider hiring someone who is no more than three years old, a particularly good age for mastering the chain of why's.

In most social and workplace environments, asking why can seem rude, since it crosses the line of generally acceptable bland and nonthreatening conversation. It is not difficult to imagine an evening out with friends in which not one thing is said that amounts to more than small talk, stuff that doesn't, in polite company, get held up to the scrutiny of "Why." Unfortunately, if we allow ourselves to be forever polite, we will never get into the habit of good thinking. We will get so used to accepting every inanity muttered near us that we will completely lose our critical faculties, and by *critical faculties* here, I do not mean to imply being critical of others. Critical faculties refers to our ability to pay close attention, to seek distinctions, to think.

Try out the why process sometime when you're with a good friend. When someone says something that puzzles you, offends you, confuses you, or just seems to be not so, simply say, "Why?" Or "Why do you think that is?" The word *why* is a wonderful dumb-conversation stopper and can often lead to probing and thoughtful conversations that work their way to underlying truth.

UNDERLYING PRINCIPLES

Once we have begun the process of trying to understand our worldview and the moral and ethical structure that we've built on these fundamental understandings, and once we have recognized that all our thinking needs to be integrated (the opposite of the condition that results in the neurosis of cognitive dissonance), we can then check whether all these are aligned with the principles that underlie the project at hand.

Decoding our own work to discover who we are is not a simple process. We are inherently blind to ourselves in many ways. Yet we must decode it so that we can check on our own work as we proceed and so that we won't end up asking others to do it for us.

THE SEARCH FOR UNIVERSALITY

When we discover that something is so, it is often useful to explore further and see whether what we have discovered is a special case or indicative of a wider truth. For instance, imagine we discover that we increase our retention of written material if we read something upside down. We might then devise a test to see if this is true for others. If it turns out to be true for others, we could then test the theory in other languages, including those that are written right to left and vertically. Then we might investigate whether inverted reading is a faster path to the brain's memory because all infants see everything upside down until their brains develop and learn to invert the image. The underlying principle might be that, since we now see everything after an inversion process by our brain, maybe that extra step slows or changes the memory pathways. Or we can look for other possible underlying principles.

We might discover that 9 is evenly divisible by 3, and that the same is true for 12, 15, 18, 45, and 111. We might notice that, when the integers in any number add up to a number divisible by 3, then the number itself is evenly divisible by 3. We can test it up into the millions, and maybe even discover a reason why these numbers work this way. Either way, this is the process of beginning to look for patterns and, eventually, an underlying universal law that connects them.

Discovering our own unique underlying principles is as complex as understanding our identity. Whereas identity is about discovering who we are, what is unique about us, and what it is we are driven to do in the world, understanding our underlying principles is about seeing "our way" of doing things. Our way of doing things is often an expression of how we think things ought to be in the world. Sometimes they're just personal and express the way we think we ought to conduct ourselves

— what we do and how we spend our time, energy, and money. But sometimes we can discover that some of "our way" is an expression not only of what we want for ourselves but also of what we think is so, in relation to the way something should be done, or the way all people should conduct themselves; or simply, we may find in some aspects of "our way" what we believe to be true.

Do your colleagues or friends call you a perfectionist? Are you casual or formal, methodical or intuitive? Do you have a tendency to "play" with things or ideas, or are you cautious? Do you believe in the inevitability of human progress, or do you believe we can easily go backward? All these aspects of personality may also reflect our beliefs about how the world works.

Discovering our underlying principles, whether about our own worldview or about a particular area in which we are developing our original thinking, is a daunting task and possibly one for which the Socratic method offers the best approach. To engage in the Socratic method requires the help of a Socrates-like friend. This friend must be learned in a very broad way, yet must be able to hold his or her own ideas and values loosely enough to be able to suspend them in order to get inside your worldview. This friend must also be able to be both inside and outside your worldview at the same time in order to see how your world fits, and differs from, a universal worldview. Your Socrates-like friend will be able to ask you the right questions to facilitate your getting to your underlying core beliefs without imposing theirs on you, and will be able to help you connect these beliefs to your complete belief system that underlies the distinctions you have made. As a result you will know what holds your beliefs together as a system, and will be able to communicate this complete system to others.

When you are able to write down your complete belief system for your worldview, to connect it together and articulate it, you will have a clear picture of what you believe to be so in the world. As you move through life, you will be able to modify, test, and refine your beliefs.

UNCOVERING ASSUMED RULES

In almost everything we develop, we will find it valuable to make explicit the assumed rules, laws, and principles that underlie our approach. If we're designing a new building, we might include among our guiding principles one that says the building will have a light footprint on the land, that it be compatible aesthetically with its neighbors, that it delight the people who pass by it and those who work there, and that it be energy efficient. If everyone involved with the building's development agrees to these principles, we will have a solid guide to check all of our developmental work against.

Artists often create rules in order to test an idea

or to stimulate their creativity by artificially limiting their choices. Schoenberg's twelve-tone system was an attempt to break the grip of the traditional major and minor scales that had dominated Western music for three centuries. Even when the audience was given an explanation of what the twelve-tone system was meant to do, it was difficult for most people to make the shift to enjoyment, since their expectations of what music should be had been set for so long. When Ernest Vincent Wright prepared to write his novel *Gadsby*, published in 1939, he tied down the letter *e* on his typewriter, challenging himself to write an entire novel without it. He announced his intent in the book's introduction, much like a tightrope artist casting a wire across a dangerous chasm.

In most creative endeavors, we set out with assumed rules simply because they fall into the category of being practical. If we're making a toaster, it must fit on a kitchen counter and be not much larger than the bread it will be toasting.

CREATING RULES

In the process of innovating, we might discover along the way that what we're doing is so new, but feels so coherent to us, that we can sense we're operating within some possibly-as-yet-unnamed rules. Imagine developing a game in which a player swings a stick at a ball that another player tries to throw past that first player who's holding the stick. We might start out saying that, if you swing at the ball and miss it, your chance is over. But that might not feel right after a while. Maybe the swinger should get more chances to hit the ball. And what about throws that are so high or low that no one can reasonably hit them? Should we count those against the number of chances the swinger gets? You can see how baseball might have evolved, with ever finer adjustments to make the game more complex, strategic, and a balance of talents.

Imagine an organization in which a large number of people are empowered to interview and hire, and that over time it becomes clear that Louise over here has some kind of gift for brilliant hiring. Almost all of her hires become highly successful in our organization, great team players but also leaders. Wouldn't it be worthwhile to discover what principles are guiding Louise in her hiring process? And once we do, and can articulate them and train others to use them, the whole organization will benefit. Finding the true bedrock underlying principles that are guiding Louise may not be easy — she might not be able to articulate them, or she may even think that what she's doing is the same as everyone else. How will we know when we've gotten to the true underlying principles? We will test them, as described in step 4 of the Endleofon. The test will be replicability. If we've discovered the true underlying principles or rules, then they can be taught to others, who will have the same success. If Louise tells us that she looks into her prospective hires' eyes and likes the way they squint when asked to solve a tough problem, that may be what's really going on, or it might not. The test of replication will tell us. Otherwise, we need to keep asking, observing, seeing, and looking for new distinctions.

CHAPTER EIGHT

{ COMPLETION }

The Alexandria Test

A genius thinker completes the work by answering two questions: Can it stand on its own? Have I provided enough additional information so that what we have innovated can be replicated or continuously improved?

O ur innovation work began by recognizing a need. Now that we seem to have completed our development work, satisfied ourselves that we have thought through our problem, tested and refined our solution, and even sought to recognize whether we might have created a new structure based on our interrelated principles, we must now think in a new way about our intended user. We must put ourselves in our user's shoes and imagine what it will be like to experience and employ what we have created.

STRUCTURAL INTEGRITY

If we're designing a bridge, or a car door, or a piton that a mountain climber is going to hang from, our handiwork had better perform as it was intended. This actually holds true for everything we innovate: our software should be bug proof, our toaster shouldn't catch on fire, our teaching system should teach. That's what structural integrity means. What we have created is complete, it hangs together, and it works not only the way we want it to but also, at the very least, the way our intended users expect it will.

Integrity means that what we have created appears to unfold in a logical way for our user. If something is necessarily strange or out of sequence, we had better give some warning in advance and make every possible effort to get our user past the learning curve. Consider the initial BMW drive-by-knob interface, in which dozens of driver controls were accessed by means of a single large knob controlling menus and submenus on the dashboard. Maybe it was great once you figured it out, but the same effort could have made you a concert pianist, as well.

Structural integrity requires that something can stand on its own — that it be complete, finished. Seeing our creation as something that the user will experience over a period of time will help us determine whether it is complete. We can look at three steps for the user that will take place in time. First there is a beginning point.

When you encounter your new product from Apple, your carefully calibrated experience begins with opening the box. We can think of the beginning point for our solar toaster as the sun's light and heat. The second step in time is an end point. With our toaster, the end point is a toasted piece of bread. If we can get our user smoothly and happily from one point to the other, we are offering something fairly complete. And there is a third requirement. We need to do whatever is necessary for user instruction, maintenance, and safety.

What about devising a better system for helping someone find a job or purchase an airplane ticket or find a mate? We need to define the beginning and end of the need we are addressing, and make sure we have connected all of the steps and possibilities along the way. If our design requires that we send our users outside of our system for some of the essential steps, have we figured out a way for them to come back and complete the process? If not, we have lost them. If, for instance, part of our job-search system requires building a database, and we send our users to a variety of websites to create or use a database, chances are we will never see them again. They will wander off without having benefited from our innovation.

In writing a book intended to help others learn something or acquire a skill, it is often a challenge for an author to know what to include and what to leave out. This is also true if we're designing a new remote control, a liberal arts curriculum, or a voting machine. If what we have created is valuable for someone, are we giving our intended users everything they need so they can get the most out of it? If everything they need is not here, are we then including referrals for the other information they will need?

THE ALEXANDRIA TEST

Aristotle was the tutor of Alexander. Soon after Alexander completed his conquest of the eastern Mediterranean, he established the library in Alexandria, Egypt. The world's leading thinkers gathered to the library a great collection of books and other written records of knowledge from across the world. Because of this unique concentration of intellectual wealth, by 300 BC Alexandria was the world center for the development of new ideas. For the next six hundred years, Alexandria was a source of light to the world, until the Roman emperor Theodosius, as part of his campaign against "paganism," ordered the library destroyed, in AD 391. Much of the world's knowledge of medicine, mathematics, history, and democracy was lost. Over the next thousand years, Europe would slip into a dark age, with the sum total of human knowledge devolving back toward ignorance. Fortunately, a few monasteries kept some of the ancient Greek and Roman texts intact, even though they were no longer studied or understood.

When the Italian Renaissance began in the middle of the 1300s, the first Renaissance thinkers rediscovered the ancient works, and from these faint embers, civilization once again flourished.

Hence this notion of the "Alexandria Test." If you learn something, and the source of your knowledge is destroyed, could you, on your own, teach others about that knowledge with enough detail, accuracy, and understanding of the underlying principles that they could in turn teach others, so that this knowledge eventually, in the hands of the right person, could be rapidly redeveloped?

For instance, imagine that the Internet has fallen away, and a global catastrophe has brought on a new Dark Age. What knowledge do you hold that would help in accelerating the next Renaissance? What could you offer about how computers and their chips were once made, so that the recovery process could leap ahead? How about your knowledge of immunology, agriculture, or the components of the alternating current (and future direct current) electrical grid?

The purpose of the Alexandria Test is not so much about preparing for a possible global catastrophe as it is about being confident that you really know or understand something. Now return to your perspective as an innovator, and consider how much you need to transfer or teach so that your work can pass the Alexandria

Test. Are you giving your colleagues, students, readers, or even users enough knowledge so that they can not only use what you are offering but also, if need be, adequately teach it to others who might in turn replicate it and build on it?

CHAPTER NINE

{ CONNECTING }

Flatten the Learning Curve

The genius thinker enters the frame of reference
of the intended user and asks, "Have I done everything
possible to ease the learning curve?"

It is our responsibility to accelerate the adoption of what we have created. Have we explored the various ways our users will grasp, understand, and employ our innovation? Have we calibrated the user's experience so that each step of the way is as intuitive, easy, and timely as possible? Are learning resources available at every possible step?

The Learning Curve

Everything new, no matter how valuable or desirable it may be, requires some effort by the intended users while learning how to use it. Whether our creation is a new digital camera, new software, our company changing the way it wants something done, or even our fabulous new solar toaster, we as creators are asking our adopter to make an effort, with the implied promise that the reward will have been worth it.

The term *learning curve* refers to a graph that plots our progress as we start to learn something. We generally start at zero and begin our climb. Most learning curves are steepest at the beginning, when everything is new and unexplored. For many of us, the hardest part often comes when we open the box of some consumer product and look at all the stuff inside. There's the gizmo itself, plus all kinds of papers and manuals that say, "Start here first," as well as offers from a range of somewhat related companies that have paid to be in the box, warranty cards, and smaller boxes holding chargers. Then there are fold-out one-page manuals, and longer, book-length manuals, sometimes hidden as PDFs on one of the installation discs.

As creators, we need to accept the fact that in many cultures most people will not read a manual. This leads to some interesting disconnects. I was recently in a U.S. Mercedes dealership that had just taken in trade a pristine one-year-old car. (Mercedes's prime market is, of course, Germany, where everyone reads the 220-page manual from cover to cover and is prepared to take a test on it.) After the customer had taken delivery of her new car, the salesman asked why she had traded so soon. It turned out that she depended on a cassette tape series, and the car didn't have a cassette player. The salesman didn't have the heart to tell her that her old car did indeed have a cassette player. All you had to do was press the button marked "Tape" and the radio-tuning dial would fold back, revealing the cassette player. How could Mercedes have done a better job of letting that buyer know there was a cassette player hidden behind the radio? A little removable tag on the radio saying "Cassette player hidden here!" might have helped.

Since we know that many people have an aversion to reading instruction manuals, even though reading manuals might be the best way to reduce the steepness of the learning curve, when we design an innovation we must also figure out how to help users overcome instruction manual phobia. Some designers do it by carefully structuring every step the purchaser takes when opening the box, with each stage explaining the next step necessary to getting the most out of the new coffee maker. The furniture company Ikea has reduced its graphics-only instructions to the greatest possible simplicity.

No matter how brilliant our creation is, we need to complete it by becoming our intended user for a time.

We must ask ourselves if we have given users everything they need to make the learning curve as gradual and easy as possible. Have we written our manuals and guides and literature in a way that lets them know we are talking to them and addressing their current state of mind and current needs?

Website design is an excellent place to check our learning-curve sensitivity. Websites for new innovations need to follow this sequence: First, we need to communicate to our visitor, "Yes! If this is your need, then you have indeed come to the right place." Second, we need to say, "This is who we are and what we stand for." Third, we need to tell the visitor, "If we are now aligned with each other, let's work together to solve your problem and make your life better. These are the steps we are going to follow" — and then we can lay out whatever will be necessary, whether it is a purchase, a trial experience, something to join, or something to do. If certain skills have to be learned, and if any of them present some difficulty, let's say so right now and explain what the level of difficulty is, how long the process will take, and what the benefits will be.

In extreme circumstances, it is not possible for the innovating organization to complete their total implementation design. Vastly complex software such as Photoshop often generates an entire training industry, and large corporate integration systems, such as SAP, have generated billions in professional services revenues. If that seems to be the case with our current innovation, we will need to plan who some of our key partners will be and to provide them with the tools and incentives to help us complete our innovation. Otherwise, our failure to adequately address this great barrier to acceptance will ensure that our innovation, no matter how valuable, will not succeed in the marketplace of ideas.

CREATING EXAMPLES

Most people love stories more than they do facts. The careful use of examples will bring your knowledge to life for your reader if you can create examples from humanity's common ground. I am often startled, when watching a Greek or Shakespearean play, by how rich the world was in its offerings of examples five hundred or even several thousand years ago. If we take our examples from the timeless, we will avoid the trap of drawing from the soon-to-be stale. Your reader two years from now probably won't know who won the *American Idol* competition last year, or recall with the same enthusiasm something you found hilarious on television last night.

Here is a short list of where to find your examples: food (including growing, hunting for, cooking, and eating); family (individuals and relationships); work (office, factory, home; repairing, building, cleaning); politics (how the community organizes and functions);

recreation; nature and the physical world; and finally, the mind. A caution regarding recreation — although many of your readers will indeed be familiar with soccer and basketball or even American football, commentators on these sports, driven by the need to fill millions of hours of airtime, have completely demolished the possibility that you will find something fresh to draw upon from them. Attempting to do so will be like calling a Hail Mary pass, stealing home, or drawing to an inside straight.

SPEAKING TO THE LISTENER

At some point we will need to communicate what we have created as a group and accelerate its adoption by others. Have we explored the various ways our audience will grasp, understand, and use this information? Have we calibrated our language and presentation for the needs of our audience?

We create because we are trying to solve a problem or pursue a new idea. Most of us are so occupied with thinking through our own thorny challenges that, when the time finally comes to take it out into the world, we are still focusing on our own issues. Have I finished this thing? Will it work the way I want it to? Will it change the world? Will our intended users understand all the hundreds of features we've built in?

In our preoccupation with all these important

issues, it can be easy to forget the other part of why we're creating: we're making something useful for others. In many ways the process of innovating requires an attempt to align two entities that are quite dissimilar — ourselves and our users. We know everything about our topic. We're experts, we're experienced, we teach it, we live it. Our identity is tied up with it. We *are* our creations occasionally.

Pity the poor user. She is eager to try this thing out, but we are in danger of talking to ourselves. We know everything about it. She knows nothing. We want to do a brain dump about every bell and whistle. She wants enough knowledge so that what we're offering can be useful to her.

For us to bridge the gap between ourselves and our intended user, we need to get in their frame of reference.

FRAME OF REFERENCE

To communicate to our users instead of to ourselves requires that we get into their shoes and heads and design our materials to provide information in a way that our imagined users would like to have the information come to them. *You* might want to discuss your new theory about teams; *they* want to know how to deal with the jerk who shows up at every important creative meeting and shoots down tender young ideas.

As you design your communication materials, you are going to imagine as many of your potential users as you can. You will want to write down portraits of half a dozen or so of them. If your product or concept is for people in a hurry, make a note of that. If they're frustrated, idealistic, anxious, or creative, you're going to keep that quality in front of you as you design your manual or instructions. You're going to think about your audience in the same way when you develop your marketing program and even your advertising — which is where you first start your conversation with your users. Imagine their current state when they begin to use your innovation, and quickly and easily let them know that you know who they are and have a pretty good notion of what's on their minds.

Write down the five to ten big questions your user is going to want answered. Ask those questions in your presentation, white paper, or FAQs. If you get those questions right, your audience will be grateful that you understood what's on their minds. And when you answer those questions, your job will be done.

Your presentation might go like this: "Putting a new roof on your house after a hurricane may not be the most fun thing you can imagine doing. But believe it or not, once you've reroofed with Acme Lock-Tight Hurricane Tiles you'll be as proud of that achievement as of anything else you've done in your life. We know you don't have time for the theory of trusses or the fascinating three-thousand-year-old history of asphalt, so this video won't waste your time. We're going to talk about safety first, before you pick up a hammer or climb a ladder. We're going to talk about the tools you'll need, some other materials you'll need to buy — and just five minutes from now, you'll be ready to go up that ladder."

"Are you talking to me?" Yes, your users will know that you're talking to them.

CHAPTER TEN

{ IMPACT }

The Point of No Return

At this stage of development, the genius thinker takes a deep breath and asks, "Where do I want to go in my life and my career?" And as a group, genius thinkers ask, "Where do we want to go together?" In developing this work, we are about to launch a creation that will eventually take on a life of its own. If this work succeeds in the marketplace, will it help us fulfill our goals?

At the beginning of this book, we considered the possibility that developing our new distinctions might be valuable to others. Now, at the end of this process, we need to reexamine our goals for this project and consider whether they are still aligned with who we are, whether our desire is to attempt to solve a problem, teach and inform others, or change the world. Now is the time to consider whether we should abort it or let it live and thrive.

Thinking and innovating can often take the shape

of a journey. We begin with our first distinction or set of ideas, and before long we might see that we have something we want to share with others. In this act of thinking and imagining, we will be creating something that will, for a while, be a part of ourselves. Eventually we will want to separate from our creation, and it might even take on a life of its own. The works that people create — buildings, paintings, companies, jet engines, symphonies, songs, books, and solar toasters — all eventually become separated from their creators.

When we initially set out to think, we may not have been thinking about this likely future separation, but at some point once again it will be worthwhile to ask ourselves what success might look like. If you are E. O. Wilson writing an encyclopedia of the ant, success might look like a global change in how ants are understood and appreciated. If you are Elisabeth Kübler-Ross writing about the stages of grieving, success might lie in having people understand that they are not alone in their suffering, and that their expectations that they will survive their grief may be comforting. If you are creating systems that will help large organizations attract and retain the most talented people, then success will be a change in the workplace for many people all over the globe.

By asking ourselves what success looks like, we can better calibrate our thinking to make sure that the work we are creating, which will eventually take on a life separate from us, reflects on us in a way that enhances our plans for our careers, our organizations, our lives.

To this point we have been talking about a strategic alignment between our innovations, our organizations, and ourselves. In some areas of innovation, at first we might not want to be overly concerned with strategic considerations. If we are working in pure research, we are likely to be pursuing our work for its own sake, no matter where it leads. Does that suggest we should ignore the strategic consequences as we continue to develop our ideas?

I don't think so. Everything we do has implications and consequences, whether we want them or not. Looking for those implications and consequences will always enrich our work, and may lead us to alter the direction of what we're doing. Imagine a scientist whose passion is to pursue some great breakthrough, such as room-temperature superconductivity. Now imagine that this scientist simply can't make progress in superconductivity, so he switches his focus for a while, to, say, nanotechnology or crystalline structures. With every test and experiment in nano or crystals, he will inevitably be looking simultaneously for clues that will be helpful in room-temperature superconducting. That kind of thinking is also strategic — moving forward in one's area of passion even when doing research in another area.

There is a third identity we need to consider here

as well, the identity of our users, the people and entities we are trying to reach with our innovations. If we are successful, will we have helped them realize their own aspirations? Have we treated them with the same level of respect that we have for ourselves and would like others to have for us as well?

The alignment of these three identities is the final test of the Endleofon process. The creators, the creation, and the impact on the intended users all need to express the same values and the same aspirations. When they do, we have achieved the grand alignment of innovation. We are on the brink of success.

Which brings us back to the effect of being aware of our identity and of where we want to go: knowing who we are transforms everything we do. Once we know where our passion lies, and what our knowledge of our identity tells us is our destiny to contribute, then everything we do will illuminate our core interests. Once we know our identity, how we use our life becomes inherently strategic.

Whenever we think and create, we are creating our greater selves. If we don't create, then what we are is limited to what we say and do and, eventually, to other people's recollections of what we said and did. By creating, we are defining a self that acts in the world and, if we desire, magnifying our contribution.

CHAPTER ELEVEN

{ ADVOCACY }

A Curator of Hooks

The genius thinker knows that the introduction of even
the greatest innovations can easily fail if left to those
who were not part of the creation. The responsibility to
develop the core communication about what has been
created begins with the creators.

W e have reached the end of the first cycle of
our work. We have looked closely at what
others have taken for granted and created
new distinctions and made them our own. We have made
the heroic effort to figure out who we are, both as individuals and, if we're working collaboratively, as a team.
We may have even lost team members in the process but
strengthened our alignment with our fellow survivors.
We have engaged in a values search, to understand our
personal values and those values implied in our work, to

make sure that what we are creating expresses what we believe to be so. We have looked at the technical and intellectual implications of our work and attempted to think about every possible consequence good and bad, knowing we can never identify all of them with certainty.

We have devised tests and models of all kinds to examine our work, and have refined our creation so that it is the best of its kind that we can presently devise. We have entered into the Great Conversation and, by carefully searching out our precedents, have also become clear on where our contribution departs from the previous state of the art. We have imagined who needs our work, not only our immediate intended user, but also those in other fields and worlds who would benefit from our discoveries. We have thought about how we might share our work with those who need it, and have even altered our development to anticipate those needs if we were able to do so.

We have contemplated success, now that we think we know what we're doing, and have checked our possible success against the measure of who we are as individuals, as team members, and as part of our organization. And we have judged, to the best of our ability, that we are happily aligned with the possibility of success.

We are at the final step of the Endleofon process. We must become advocates.

THE THIRD REVOLUTION

Now the hard part. The marketplace for innovation is an imperfect one. You may have indeed created a breakthrough solar toaster. You may have completed a pneumatic system so overwhelmingly logical that UPS ought to be standing outside your door along with delegates from the U.S. Patent office. But it usually doesn't work this way.

The term for the spread of better ideas is *diffusion of innovation*. There is a classic textbook by that name, and in its studies of various farmers' adoption of hybrid corn in the 1930s the term *early adopters* was first used.

There have been three technological revolutions in the history of diffusion. The first was the advent of writing and the rise of written history, around 4000 BC. Modern civilization followed. The next was the invention of movable type by Gutenberg, around 1439, which took written history a step forward by making the production of books, and therefore the diffusion of innovation, vastly less expensive. The Renaissance followed. We are in the midst of the third great revolution in the diffusion of innovation, and that is, of course, the Internet. Now the flow of innovation can be global, instantaneous, and cheap. With these ingredients, we should soon witness a new age in which ignorance is rapidly reduced and civilization makes great strides.

What, then, remains as the great barrier to the acceptance of our breakthrough? If we really have made something of potential value to others, why doesn't the world always beat a path to our door? Among the many answers are: peoples' reluctance to change unless there is an overwhelming need, the difficulty people have in letting go of current beliefs, the challenge of the learning curve, and the busyness of everyday life that doesn't leave a lot of time or energy for adopting something new, even if it's an improvement. All of these, though, fall within the general challenge of communication.

SPAN OF DEPARTURE

We need to define what we have created in the precise way we want it to be perceived by others. We must take the first cut at defining our creation.

Modest improvements are not all that difficult to introduce. Bigger! Faster! Less salt! Less glutinous! What about major innovations? They are vastly more difficult because, with great innovations, we have usually pushed outside the frame of reference of our intended users. If you're already using Photoshop 8.0, you can probably appreciate what's new in 8.5. But what if I'm asking you to trade in your car for a two-wheeled scooter?

I measure the distance from what our intended user already knows, or currently employs, to acceptance of our innovation, with a concept I call the *span of departure*.

I mean to suggest a dock and a rowboat. When that rowboat is tied up tight to the dock, it's not too hard to get in the rowboat from the dock. But let that rope run out a few feet and, suddenly, trying to make it into that little boat is going to take a pretty great leap. Yes, it seems like a cute little boat, but I'm not sure it's worth getting soaked to find out just how cute.

The greater the span of departure of our innovation, the more difficult will be its successful introduction. We will need great endorsements, success stories, metaphors, and trial experiences. And we will need to discover the urgent needs of our intended users that will help them make that leap off the dock.

Einstein created a world of thought that departed so radically from the then-current state of the art that physicists today believe that Einstein, on his own, moved human knowledge forward a hundred years. His work could easily have remained impenetrable to others, but the second and necessary part of Einstein's genius was his ability to create visual images, narratives, and metaphors that helped others grasp his vast departures. To explain relativity, he talked about two people with two watches on two trains that were traveling in opposite directions. If one train was going extremely fast, the watch on that person's wrist would slow down compared to the watch on the other person's wrist. If the train were to approach the speed of light, the person on that train would age much more slowly than the person on the slower train. Einstein could almost make you feel as if you understood relativity. If we are to be geniuses in innovation, we must also be geniuses in developing our advocacy tools.

Advocacy Hooks

If we value what we have created and feel it would be of benefit to others, then it is necessary that everyone who created this work commit to working for its successful introduction. It is our responsibility to explain what value we have created and not to rely on others to figure it out for themselves. Have we discovered the advocacy hooks that will help people understand as quickly as possible the value we have created? Can we communicate that value to others in an unforgettable way?

In working recently with a client on a book about managing not-for-profit organizations so that they achieve and maintain financial health, I saw that my client had a list of dozens of items that board members needed to know. I found one of those items unusually compelling: My client had identified a little-known syndrome called the zone of insolvency, which, it turned out, most nonprofits drift in and out of. Many get stuck in the zone, eventually winding down or going broke. The shock was that many millions of people who volunteered to serve on nonprofit boards didn't know they might have financial responsibility if the organization they were helping suddenly went broke or got into some other difficulty. We decided to elevate the zone: it went from simply being an interesting fact to being the urgent driver of everything else in the book. The threat of falling into the zone became the central, urgent idea behind keeping nonprofits financially robust, and we named the book *The Zone of Insolvency*.

In the process of making our distinctions and thinking through their implications, we also need to be looking for the intriguing bits of information that will pique the interest of others and make them want to learn more. Such advocacy hooks are priceless because, if we can find them, they will greatly enhance our ability to get others interested in our ideas. Advocacy hooks can also be found in achievements or in scientific results that bring us credibility. One of the first things we must do when opening the process of introducing ideas into the world is to establish our legitimacy as the bearer of these ideas. If we have evolved a new process for something, the fact that we have achieved a 70 percent success rate might be meaningful to our audience. Sometimes an endorsement by someone who is well known and credible in our field can help speed the acceptance of what we have to say.

Searching for advocacy hooks throughout our thinking and development process will, from the very beginning, help us organize our work and communicate what we are thinking about. When the time comes to present a speech, write a briefing for the sales force, complete your book, or run a demo, these hooks will be essential for helping others understand and get involved in what you have discovered.

I MUST STAND FOR WHAT I HAVE CREATED

It is important to have made valuable discoveries, yet if we complete all the steps in the Endleofon process except for this final one, we cannot be confident that we have made our contribution to the world of ideas. We must learn to be the advocate for our ideas, to champion their testing and adoption by others. Just as our work is an expression of us, we must be the supporters of our work.

The world is made better through the dissemination and adoption of better ideas. When we think of human progress, generally this is what we are thinking about. Why is it that new and better ideas don't spread around the globe soon after they are first articulated? One of the reasons may be a lack of advocacy.

When I was still in my teens I was attracted to a book in my father's law library titled *The Art of Advocacy*, and I read it through. Some books sink into us and become part of how we act in the world, even though we forget the book itself. Many years later, when it dawned on me that I was in fact an advocate for ideas, I remembered the title of the book and, thanks to abebooks.com, soon had a comfortably worn copy in my hands. I dove in to see what, if anything, had inspired me decades before. The book, by Lloyd Stryker, is comprised of portraits of great criminal lawyers engaged in the various stages of preparing for and conducting trials. What stands out is the tremendous courage of the great advocates. After all the expert testimony and eyewitness accounts and physical evidence, the stark reality is that, often, the only instrument standing between the client and death is the language created by the advocate for his final argument to the jury.

When I first begin to work with a business thinker or other innovator, I ask questions and read the client's materials to see what is new and valuable. As our work progresses, I look for advocacy hooks, the bits and pieces that will help me sell their ideas at some future point. Often, the advocacy hooks that I uncover in the first hours of conversation end up in a book proposal, on the flap copy, and on the back of the finished book.

Buckminster Fuller was a walking, talking advocacy hook for his ideas throughout his life. He constantly searched for new language to make sure that the breakthrough nature of his ideas would not be confused with old ideas. As an early environmentalist, he was able to shift perception about our planet by calling it Spaceship Earth. Suddenly we were all in this together. When he created his car in 1933 or piloted his factory-built housing, he used his all-encompassing term *Dymaxion*.

He made films of each discovery so that, decades before television, people could see his inventions in action.

When high school students are assigned to write papers and present them to their classmates, they will often get interested in the project when something in their research touches them. Maybe they'll find a drawing of how people were stacked in a slave ship, or read a letter from Lincoln to a young girl. Maybe the lyric of a song will capture their imagination, or a story from several centuries past will come alive for them. These advocacy hooks become the secret ingredients of successful communication, and when the students present their discoveries, they will be able to do so with excitement and passion.

You can imagine how important these things are for attorneys preparing a case. Johnny Cochran, O. J. Simpson's attorney during his murder trial, got Simpson off with a single advocacy hook: "If it doesn't fit, you must acquit."

When Louis Pasteur was developing his live rabies virus (made from the spinal cord of a rabid animal) an assistant accidentally pricked himself with a virus-laden instrument. The vaccine against rabies was still in the early stages of development, but the assistant needed an inoculation right away. Pasteur ordered that he, too, be inoculated. Although no assistant would inject the great man, two other assistants joined in the experiment and were injected. Fortunately, everyone survived, and the story helped spread the news of the rabies vaccine. But perhaps the greatest hook, one that thrilled the public of the day, were the stories of Pasteur's great personal courage. When he needed to extract saliva from a rabid bulldog, to keep his hands free he held the collecting tube with his teeth while his assistants wearing heavy leather gloves held the dog down.

It's not enough just to have an idea or care about a cause. The world is full of brilliant ideas left undeveloped and noble causes abandoned. To make a difference in the world ultimately requires understanding how to be an advocate for your ideas or causes. You can have the most important or best idea, one with the potential to make a big difference in people's lives, but without your advocacy even your greatest work will run the risk of not being disseminated.

{ THE ENDLEOFON QUESTIONS }

In order to develop our innovations to their highest possible level and to facilitate their acceptance by the people who would benefit most from our creations, we need to answer all of the following eleven questions.

1. DISTINCTIONS

What do I see? New ideas are the result of perceiving new distinctions.

2. IDENTITY

Who am I? Why are these ideas important to me, and why am I driven to share them with the world? Have I made my identity clear to my audience so they know where I am coming from?

3. Implications

Where do my ideas lead? If what I am saying is true, then what are all the consequences I can imagine?

4. Testing

What am I blind to? Have I imagined how my ideas might impact a variety of situations, places, and people? Have I questioned everything about my assumptions? What would prove me wrong? Can I create a model of my work and find precise analogues?

5. Precedent

Who else has seen something like this? By asserting that I have something to say, I am entering into the Great Conversation of ideas that stretches back through the centuries. We cannot know everything that has been said about our area of focus before we began our work, but we must try to be aware of important, precedent thought.

6. Need

Who needs this knowledge? If what I am saying is so, for whom would this knowledge be valuable? This question forces us out of focusing solely on our own area and may lead us to find the universals in our thinking. Understanding who needs us most will also help us in crafting what we say.

7. FOUNDATION

Are there underlying principles? What is the world I'm working in? What are the underlying values expressed here? What are the applicable rules or structures that obtain here? Can I pull these together into a coherent group or body of law?

8. COMPLETION

Is everything here? If this idea or product is valuable for someone, am I giving my audience everything they need for it to be useful? If everything they need is not here, have I explained what other information they will need in order to know enough to take action or teach others?

9. CONNECTING

Who am I addressing? Do I understand my audience's frame of reference? Am I writing for my reader, speaking to my listener, carefully guiding the experience of my user?

10. IMPACT

Where do I want to go? In creating this work I have launched an alter ego that will eventually take on a life of its own. If this development or body of knowledge succeeds in the marketplace of ideas, will it help me fulfill my goals for my life? Are the identities of the creators, the creation, and the users aligned?

11. ADVOCACY

Am I supporting the adoption of my ideas? My thinking stands for me. Now I must stand for what I have created.

{ ACKNOWLEDGMENTS }

This book is dedicated to Leanne, the love of my life. Our endless, continuous dialogue makes life not only delightful but also carefully examined.

Thank you to everyone at New World Library, who fundamentally helped shape the book into its current and highly useful form, and especially to Jason Gardner, my editor, for his superb editorial contribution and his enthusiasm for the potential of this book.

I can still see my grandfather Henry Tabakin, "Gop" to us, as he practiced dentistry in and around Cleveland, Ohio, more than fifty years ago — with the odd articulated drilling machine with its driving cables running up both sides of the arms, the porcelain plate that held his tools, the open blue flame for in-the-moment sterilization. Busy with his patient as he seemed to be, in reality his dentistry barely distracted him from his real work, which was thinking seriously about some

Talmudic issue he had selected for himself that day. A great scholar, he had been the youngest rabbi ordained at the legendary Telz Yeshiva in Lithuania. He was a radical who shunned orthodoxy of any kind. In America he was in love with the idea of the country: he invented and invested in inventions, he traded stocks, he read Walter Lippmann with great respect. He eventually wrote a book that has been a family treasure down through our generations.

My grandmother would criticize him for never letting me win at chess. She thought it was harsh. He simply observed that, if and when I won, I would know that the victory was legitimate. Eventually I did, and I still savor the moment.

My grandfather delighted in the exercise of pure reason. Once a week, on Friday nights, he would share with us the moral or ethical puzzle he had been thinking about, and after giving us his thoughts, he would invite my sister, Laura; my brother, Ivan; and me to reason with him and see what our thinking might produce. This set the tone for family life at our table. My parents were both English teachers, and my father had gone to law school nights and summers, eventually practicing law with his two brothers. Mom was an in-demand book reviewer in Cleveland, in the days when the book reviewer's job was to report on important books to large groups of people, only a few of whom would actually read the book themselves. Dad was an unusually wise man — a passionate advocate for justice in and out of the courtroom, a gentle teacher, a hysterical mimic who shared with us the best jokes of the day, many of which entered into my family culture and even that of my children.

Our table every night was a forum for topics of the day, laughs, fights, and inspiration. My brother, two years my senior, is a brilliant and contrarian thinker, and often baited me into difficult debates with his outrageous premises. I learned never to debate with him unless I had my facts straight, or he'd know in a second I was on wobbly ground. Out of necessity I became an expert in the just-in-time killer fact, some even based on the truth.

I have been particularly fortunate in the talented and brilliant clients who have chosen to work with me over the last twenty years. With each project I have had to learn a whole new universe — the client's area of expertise. Whether tackling theories of change management, constraint theory, or human brain development, I have been privileged to be at the top of the thought chain in world after world. I am grateful for each of my clients, for the opportunity to help, and for the gift of their distinctions. I am grateful for the relationships that have developed into treasured friendships, especially with Chris Barr and Dr. Jim Taylor and their wonderful families, who have become part of ours, and ours part of theirs.

I must single out one client for special thanks. Lawrence Ackerman was an early client, which was fortunate for me and for my clients who followed, because his discoveries and insights into human and corporate identity have changed my life and made a fundamental contribution to my methodology. Everything I do is infused with the natural laws of identity that he discovered.

Special thanks to John Buydos, science reference librarian at the Library of Congress, for his research on the Wright Brothers' wind tunnel and their correspondence.

I am filled with gratitude and joy for my four sons, Joshua, Milo (and his wife, Thuy), David (and his fiancée, Helen), and Maxwell, and for my brother and sister and their mates, for their sharing their brilliant thinking and work with me throughout our lives. When I think of the joy of playing with ideas, I am always inspired by the wit and wisdom of my cousin Dr. LeRoy Shaw, who has been like an older brother since the days when he arrived in Cleveland for his medical residency. These are the core people with whom I have engaged in dialogue at dinners over the years, in a floating salon in Leanne's and my household and in theirs. These dinners have been the drivers of my intellectual life.

The love of pure thought that began with our beloved Gop and his optimism about the future of humankind continues to illuminate our lives and this book.

{ INDEX }

{ ABOUT THE AUTHOR }

Gerald Sindell is the founder of Thought Leaders International, a firm that guides leaders and organizations of all kinds to maximize their return on the most precious capital of all: their ideas. Sindell works with such corporate clients as Yahoo! and Accenture, as well as with leading business and psychology authors. Sindell worked as a Hollywood film director before turning to book publishing. As a book developer, editor, and eventually the founder and publisher of Tudor Publishing and Knightsbridge Publishing, Sindell has helped shape many books and careers, having put more than 75 million books in print. He speaks to audiences throughout the world and is represented by the Bright Sight Group at www.bright sightgroup.com. Sindell lives in Tiburon, California. His website is www.thoughtleadersintl.com.